The FLYING DOCTORS

James Oram was born in New Zealand and has worked on newspapers and magazines in London, Melbourne and Sydney. For twenty years he covered major stories in Australia, the South Pacific and Asia. Now a resident of Sydney, he is the author of six books, ranging from a biography of Pope John Paul II to a look behind the scenes of the incredibly successful soap, *Neighbours*. Soap operas are his relaxation.

Other books by James Oram:

The Business of Pop

The Hellraisers (with Jim Fagan)

The People's Pope

Hogan: The Story of a Son of Oz

Neighbours: Behind the Scenes

Home and Away: Behind the Scenes

The FLYING DOCTORS

The Inside Story

JAMES ORAM

with additional material by Terry Blake

BBC BOOKS

*This book is dedicated to the late Hector Crawford,
without whom there may not have been an
Australian television production industry.*

Many people helped with this book, including members of the cast of *The Flying Doctors* and staff of Crawford Productions. A special thanks goes to Terry Blake who researched and compiled so much of it.

(Main photo), Horizon International, photo Glenn Gibson
(Inset left),London Features International
(Inset right and back cover), The Nine Network, Australia.

PICTURE CREDITS

Auscape International 44; Courtesy Australia House 40; Courtesy Australian News and Information Bureau 21, 24, 29, 31, 32; © BBC 73; British Film Institute 107, 114; Camera Press, photo George Lipman 27; Courtesy The Commonwealth Institute 34; Courtesy Hodder and Stoughton 22; Hulton Deutsch Collection 9, 37; Courtesy Independent Television 77; The Kobal Collection 52, 58, 59; London Features International 70, 72, 75, 79 and colour section page 6; © New South Wales Printing Office 13; Solo/News Ltd, Australia 54, 71, 85 (right), 87, 91, 92, 103 and colour section pages 2, 3, 8, 9; All other pictures © The Nine Network, Australia.

Published by BBC Books,
a division of BBC Enterprises Limited,
Woodlands, 80 Wood Lane, London W12 0TT
First Published 1991
© James Oram 1991
ISBN 0 563 36217 0
Designed by Peartree Design Associates
Set in Aster by Ace Filmsetting Ltd, Frome
Printed and bound in Great Britain by Clays Ltd, St Ives Plc
Colour separations by Dot Gradations Ltd, Chelmsford
Cover printed by Clays Ltd, St Ives Plc

CONTENTS

CAST OF THE SERIES (in alphabetical order)

Character	Role in Series	Actor
George Baxter	Unpopular local grazier	Bruce Barry
Vic Buckley	Local publican	Maurie Fields
Nancy Buckley	Runs local pub with husband, Vic	Val Jallay
Dr Tom Callaghan	Original Flying Doctor	Andrew McFarlane
Nick Cardaci	Likeable young odd-job man	Alex Papps
Violet Carnegie	Beloved town matriarch	Pat Evison
Sgt Jack Carruthers	Coopers Crossing police sergeant	Terry Gill
Demetris Goannidis (DJ)	Radio operator at RFDS base	George Kapiniaris
Sharon Herbert	Aboriginal teenager	Kylie Belling
Luke Mitchell	Drifter and part-time publican	Gerard Kennedy
Hurtle Morrison	Garage mechanic	Max Cullen
Sam Patterson	RFDS pilot who marries Emma Plimpton	Peter O'Brien
Emma Plimpton	Mechanic who marries pilot, Sam Patterson	Rebecca Gibney
Dr Chris Randall	Female Flying Doctor	Liz Burch
Dr David Ratcliffe	Young Flying Doctor learning the ropes	Brett Climo
Dr Geoff Standish	Takes over from Dr Tom Callaghan; marries Kate Wellings	Robert Grubb
Sister Kate Wellings	Flying Doctor nurse who weds Dr Geoff Standish	Lenore Smith

MINYIP

Even before he forced open his eyes, Lofty Dugan groped for a can of beer. One, at least, had to be in the back of the station-wagon where he had rolled out his swag blankets for the night. After a hearty session on the grog he never went to sleep without a can or two for the morning; the day had to be kick-started into life somehow and he hadn't yet found a better way than a beer. His hand found a can of Victoria Bitter, a warm can but, what the heck, an old Holden station-wagon does not come equipped with a refrigerator. He opened his eyes, pulled off the tab and swallowed its contents in a few gulps.

'*Ahhhh,*' he exhaled and belched loudly and satisfyingly. For a moment or two he wondered where he was and then remembered he was outside a town called Minyip. He didn't know Minyip from a hole in the ground, having only selected the place from a signpost. But a quick check of the map in his mind showed it was roughly where he hoped it would be, that is, on the edge of the Little Desert, the Wimmera region, in western Victoria and therefore between Melbourne and Adelaide. He had been to Melbourne to visit a mate, staying only a couple of nights because big cities were not his cup of tea (or rather his can of beer), and now wanted to get to Adelaide to see his parents – and maybe have a flutter at the casino which had a two-up game. Lofty reckoned if he couldn't win at two-up he was a mug beyond salvation. He had the time and he had the money.

Lofty was a gun shearer. Some say he was, and maybe still is, one of the best around with a blade. Like other shearers he travelled the country skimming the greasy wool from the backs of Australia's 200 million sheep and had just finished at a big station up north. His wallet was full, he had been thirsty and the signpost to a town called Minyip was a siren's call.

The moment he saw Minyip he liked it. The town was a comfortable

size, which meant it was occupied by less than 1000 people. He liked the wide main street, the old shop fronts with their wooden verandahs and peeling advertisements for Bushell's Tea, forgotten brands of sauce and remarkable potions slumped beneath rusting corrugated iron roofs. He liked the Club Hotel better.

Climbing out of the station-wagon, Lofty stretched, yawned, scratched, took a leak and rolled a cigarette from the contents of a pouch made from a bull's scrotum. He drew heavily on the tobacco which caused him to cough like an old tractor trying to start its engine on a cold morning and then grinned as he remembered the evening in the pub. He had started with schooners of beer, graduated to schooners with rum chasers and had finally thrown down a few brandies for medicinal purposes. He had got talking to a couple of old-timers and then a chain-hand from a well-boring rig had intruded wanting to argue about sheep.

Lofty hadn't wanted to argue with anyone, but the chain-hand had persisted.

'Bloody dopey animals,' the chain-hand said. 'You'd have to be a mug to work 'em.'

Lofty knew sheep were not candidates for Mensa but was not going to admit it, especially to a dumb chain-hand from a well-boring rig. 'Smarter than you, which ain't saying much,' he said. 'Know what a sheep can do? A sheep can grow one and a half pounds of wool a month, enough to make four men's suits a year. Only thing you can grow is bullshit.'

A fight would have developed had not the chain-hand taken another look at the shearer and understood he was not called Lofty because he had worked in pantomime with Snow White. Wisely the chain-hand decided a song was in order. Lofty joined in when the chain-hand bellowed the old shearers' anthem, *Flash Jack from Gundagai*:

> *I've shore at Burrabogie, and I've shore at Toganmain. . .*
> *All among the wool boys, all among the wool,*
> *Keep your wide blades full, boys, keep your wide blades full.*
> *I can do a respectable tally myself whenever I like to try,*
> *But they know me round the backblocks as Flash Jack from*
> *   Gundagai. . .*

And that is all Lofty remembered until he woke next morning in his station-wagon parked on a dirt track a few miles from Minyip. After rolling up his swag, he started the station-wagon and headed towards the town, hoping to find a cafe serving breakfast. He drove past wheat fields stretching to the horizon, and into the main street.

But this wasn't Minyip. Minyip had disappeared.

As he said later, recounting the tale: 'Fair go, I thought I was in the horrors. The buildings looked much the same, y'know; the pub was in the same place. So was the bank and the store. I remembered them when I drove in the night before. But it was a totally different place. I'm tellin' you, I wouldn't have been surprised to see purple snakes. It was almost enough to make a man give up the booze.'

A Flying Doctor arrives in a deserted region of the outback to help an unfortunate bushman

The first thing he saw which hadn't been there the previous day was a war memorial slap bang in the middle of the crossroads in the main street. He almost ran into it. Then he noticed that the Club Hotel no longer existed. It still had the wide verandah with iron lace girding the first floor, but now it was called the Majestic. The bank, where he hoped to cash a cheque, was no longer in the same state. Yesterday it was the State Bank of Victoria; now it was the State Bank of New South Wales. And, stone the crows, even the cars had New South Wales number plates when they should have carried Victorian registration numbers.

To make matters worse, people were bustling about as though they had important business on their minds. People didn't bustle in country towns unless the pub was on fire. The pub was not on fire; it only had a different name. And the people, they had changed from sauntering bushies in wide-brimmed hats to townies in designer shirts and jeans and sunglasses. For Christsakes, even the street names appeared to have changed.

But more horrors were to come. He saw a signpost with directions to Alice Springs. Now, even in his befuddled state, he knew Alice Springs wasn't just up the road. It was 1000 miles away, in the middle of Australia, not on the plains of western Victoria.

Maybe he had died. He thought it worth checking out to see if he was in heaven, hell, or someplace in between, and stopped a passing stranger.

'What's goin' on?'

The stranger squinted at him, his hands in the pockets of a greasy overall. 'What do you mean, what's going on?'

'Where's Minyip?'

'Right here. This is Minyip.'

'No it's not. When I crashed out it was Minyip. Now it's somewhere else.'

The stranger threw back his head and burst into laughter. Lofty, deciding he was the target of some joke he couldn't fathom, thrust out his chest like a pouter pigeon. He was a six foot two inches pouter pigeon with a bad hangover.

'What's so bloody funny?' he demanded urgently.

The man in the overall shook his head. 'You a stranger?'

The metamorphosis of Minyip: the production team interrupt the quiet, little-known outback town to film an episode for the series

'Just got in yesterday.'

'Well, you're still in Minyip all right, mate. But today it's Coopers Crossing. This is where we make *The Flying Doctors* television series.'

Lofty shook his head, now in a state of utter confusion. 'Look, lemme buy you a beer so you can tell me I'm not mad.'

And that is how actor Max Cullen, who played the part of garage mechanic Hurtle Morrison in the series, came to be drinking at an indecent hour of the day with gun shearer Lofty Dugan. Max could sympathise with Lofty's confusion. He had seen it often when strangers came to Minyip and, bewildered, found they were in Coopers Crossing. Sometimes, when waiting for takes outside his fictional garage, he had been approached by passing motorists demanding petrol. A few had got indignant when he had to tell them that not only could he not supply petrol but he couldn't even give them a burst of free air. 'I'm taking this up with your head office,' said one who had the look of a travelling salesman. Because Max was not fond of salesmen, travelling or not, he suggested the man have sexual congress with himself.

'We called it the metamorphosis of Minyip,' said Max.

Every three weeks Minyip became Coopers Crossing to provide exterior shots for the series. It had the look and feel of an outback town, although it was only four hours drive from Melbourne, with a bigger town, Horsham, close enough to provide accommodation for actors and crew.

Lofty Dugan was not the only stranger confused by the town's overnight change. Tom Murphy, the local newsagent, remembered a commercial traveller who slept in his car on the edge of town: 'He had business in the place next day. He woke up and the first thing he saw was the sign Coopers Crossing. He rubbed his eyes and thought he had gone mental.'

The news agency didn't help the disturbed state of the commercial traveller. Leaning against his shop's front wall were posters for Sydney newspapers.

Another tale concerned a farmer who hadn't been to town for a long time. He saw a sign on a building stating it was the Municipal Chambers. In fact it was an old bank building, now a private residence. The farmer walked in and demanded that the householder, whom he took to be the shire clerk, do something about the appalling condition of the road near his farm, and be quick about it.

Minyip is an Aboriginal word for ashes. Oscar Whitbread, the series producer, was not privy to this fact when he first saw Minyip. He only knew it was exactly what he wanted. Minyip sits in a vast expanse of wheatfields, a checkerboard of gold, brown and green. 'I'm damned lucky to have found it . . . before Peter Weir did a *Witness*,' he said, referring to the Australian director's movie about the Amish community in Pennsylvania. Minyip is not an Amish town, however, but strongly Lutheran; its townsfolk descendants of the German settlers of the 1870s.

The town has not fared well in recent years. It once had a population of 850. Today it has around 500, the empty shop fronts are reminders of better times when farms were smaller and employed the entire family. They grew, became more mechanised and the young folk moved to the cities. When Minyip was chosen as the location for *The Flying*

A typical outback town, photographed in the early 1900s

Doctors, the population quietly celebrated even though filming could sometimes be a pain in the neck with disruptions to everyday life. 'We had a very nice relationship but we had to watch ourselves because film crews can take over,' said Whitbread. 'The town was terribly patient with us.'

The townsfolk sometimes grumbled because of the inconvenience. In the case of a town the size of Minyip, inconvenience is measured by having to walk a few yards instead of parking the car anywhere along the wide main street. But the grumbling stopped when the cash tills started ringing. 'I think it did a lot of good for the town,' said Lyn Schurmann, a farmer's wife. 'Some people were disgruntled. They couldn't park in front of the shops or walk where they wanted to and couldn't lead the life they'd been leading – a very quiet life.'

The proprietor of the general store, Frank Pryor, agreed. 'Whenever you've got a project like this you'll get knockers. But in this case I'd

say the knockers were far outnumbered by those who appreciated *The Flying Doctors* being here.' When scenes were shot outside the pub, Frank Pryor often came down in his white apron to catch some of the action. 'I can watch the shop from here,' he said.

It was that kind of town.

Some locals earned a little on the side by appearing as extras. Herb Krause got to be a television star at the age of eighty-two; his role to sit outside the pub with his walking stick. He was on the credits as Old Codger 2, the number 1 Old Codger an extra imported from Melbourne. 'A bloke ought to be proud of himself. I was the only bloke in town with his name on the credits. The others didn't give me a hard time. Just sometimes when I went to the Senior Citizens' Club they'd say, "Here comes the fillum star."' The club building itself had become the Flying Doctors' base complete with flagpole, signs and radio mast.

George Clark, who had been in Minyip all his sixty-eight years, didn't mind the regular invasion, either. 'Specially the young girl actors and their lovely legs,' he confessed. 'Cheered me up no end. I liked talking to the boys, young Andrew (McFarlane) and Lewis (Fitzgerald). I'd always been a bugger to talk to. If the weather was reasonable, I never missed comin' to watch. It's the greatest thing ever to happen to Minyip.'

The metamorphosis of Minyip took place overnight. The good folk went to sleep in the town they had known all their lives and woke up in Coopers Crossing. Signs were fixed to buildings, although some stayed permanently. Jack was wheeled out and placed in the middle of the crossroads. Jack was the war memorial, an obelisk on which stood a statue of a soldier, the sort of monument found in most country towns, except this one was made from polystyrene and chipboard. Each night Jack (no one knew why it was called Jack) was wheeled away in case it was demolished by a passing truck. 'It was wiped out three times when we first started shooting here . . . residents kept crashing into it,' said Chris Page, production manager. A band rotunda was built. It was a rather nice rotunda so the residents agreed it should stay. Now they sit there in the sun waiting for something to happen.

But filming in Minyip caused one uncomfortable problem. Australia is sometimes mistakenly thought of as a country where the climate rivals that of Hades. And so it can be, in the outback, where the

Lenore Smith as Sister Kate Wellings and Liz Burch as Dr Chris Randall on set for an episode of *The Flying Doctors*

temperature often goes beyond 100 degrees. Minyip, on the other hand, can be freezing, especially when the wind howls off the plains slicing through the light clothing worn by the actors who, of course, were dressed for heat. 'There was sleet in '23,' Herb Krause remembered, 'but I've never seen snow.'

Pamela Bone, a reporter for the *Melbourne Age* newspaper, watched the cast pretending to be in the searing outback when in fact the temperature was around zero. 'For the actor, Liz Burch, the reality of making the scene was nearly as big a test of courage as the scene was supposed to portray,' Bone wrote. 'Although most people are under the illusion that film and television people lead interesting and glamorous lives, there is absolutely nothing glamorous about being drenched with a fire hose, while at the same time being almost blown off your feet by a wind machine . . .'

Most actors in *The Flying Doctors* have had to go through the pretence that the temperature is scorching hot when in truth it's the middle of winter. Marcus Graham, a twenty-six-year-old actor, was filming on location when it was six degrees. To add to his misery he had to look as though he was sweating in summer heat. 'So they sprayed me with sweat as I wandered around in a singlet nearly freezing to death,' he recalled.

After the initial mini-series and a couple of years of filming the weekly series, Minyip became known as the town that was base for *The Flying Doctors*. Tourists arrived to see the action, as many as 300 on long holiday weekends, drawn by the fantasy they saw on the small screen. Sometimes they got upset if the fantasy didn't measure up to the truth.

'Yeah, they'd come in here and want to know where old Vic was . . . still do as a matter of fact,' said Gerry Fullerton, licensee of the Club Hotel. Vic Buckley (played by Maurie Fields) is the Coopers Crossing publican. 'I'd say he's gone on holiday for a couple of weeks. Some of them don't seem to know the difference between what's happening on the screen and real life.'

The Club Hotel was turned into the Majestic Hotel for the series. Only the exterior of the building was used and occasionally shots of the stairs, the balcony and bedrooms. The interior was built in the studio. 'Some are a bit disappointed the interior's not the same, but give them a couple of drinks and they're happy,' said Fullerton. 'Then they want to know where the Old Codgers are. Well, Herb's in a wheelchair now and can't get around very much.'

The tourists were welcomed by the small business community, if not the television crew. 'The crew reckoned the tourists interfered with them, asking the actors for autographs, getting in the road a bit,' said Tom Murphy. 'But they were good for us, popping into the shop and buying things. The show put Minyip on the map.'

Some of the more enterprising inhabitants traded on Coopers Crossing. A souvenir shop opened, selling such desirable items as locally composed poems printed and blown up for wall hangings, post cards, posters and tea towels, made by members of the local Historical Society. 'Actually, we did quite well out of them,' said Lyn Schurmann.

Then came a decision that ended Minyip's schizophrenic existence. Crawford Productions, the producers, and the Nine Network, which screens the series, saw the costs increasing until they were over A$200 000 an episode, a considerable sum for a country of around five

On location in Minyip

million households. Seventy per cent of each episode involved exterior shots which Oscar Whitbread had, in the earlier days, described as 'demanding and very brave'. Cast and crew had to be accommodated and transport provided. The costs were too high and the series was switched to a Melbourne studio with exterior shots closer to the city. No one liked the change, except perhaps the actors who no longer had to perform in the depths of winter on Minyip's wind-swept main street while pretending the weather was so hot you could fry eggs on the pavement. Some miss the quaintness of a country town where time may not have stopped but where at least the pace of life was slower than the rest of the world: the cake shop with its notice-board carrying messages for lost sheep, the visit of a travelling dental mechanic; a fancy dress afternoon at the pre-school and a night at the local hall with the theme *Where were you when the ship went down*, Rowan's haberdashery shop where they still have items marked in pounds,

17

shillings and pence, even though Australia went decimal thirty years ago. They miss a part of Australia that is fading.

And the crew had enjoyed working not only on location but with film instead of videotape. 'You're not stuck in the studio all the time and you have real sunlight and lovely strong images that you can get out of film and from being out on location so much,' said Ron Hagen, one of the directors of photography. 'I think it added a lot more.'

The crew returns to Minyip every now and then to shoot some exteriors. 'But all they do is scoot around a bit, film the pub, the hall,' said Tom Murphy. 'It's not the same. Minyip will never be the same again.'

But the fans still arrive, at least three coach loads each Sunday. 'We give them a sausage, a bit of cake, a cup of tea and they take a look around,' said Tom Murphy. He has a visitors' book in his shop containing more than 2000 names. Many are from New Zealand, Britain and Europe.

'We get a tremendous number of visitors, especially from the Netherlands, and a fair share from England as well,' said Gerry Fullerton. 'They break their holidays in Melbourne to come up and see the town. As a matter of fact there's some English people turning up in a few weeks. We had an American here, he lived in The Hague. He stayed at the pub for a couple of nights and had a marvellous time.'

For several reasons, none of which would pass an academic test, the Netherlands has taken to *The Flying Doctors* in much the same way Britain has embraced the soapie, *Neighbours*. It soon became one of their top rating programmes. One reason for its success might lie in the difference between the two countries, in particular the feeling of space. In Australia there are cattle stations bigger than the Netherlands, country cops have beats covering more territory than Belgium. And then there's the weather. The show's story editor, Andrew Kennedy, put it this way: 'If you were sitting in a bedsitter in Putney with twenty pence in the meter and about four inches of ice and snow on the window-sill, wouldn't you want to watch Lenore Smith sauntering around the outback?'

Minyip has now all but lost its identity. It's not sure whether it is Minyip, Coopers Crossing or a studio set. Maybe it's all three. Visitors searching for the town ask for directions to Coopers Crossing, not Minyip, and the locals, aware that they're onto a good thing, keep up the pretence. Many of the buildings still carry Coopers Crossing signs, including the grand colonial edifice of the Club Hotel, built in 1905. It remains the Majestic. An old horse bazaar had been done up to look like a garage, the same one where Max Cullen used to argue with confused tourists and travellers.

'One lady from England, she couldn't believe there was such a building as Emma's garage,' said Lyn Schurmann. 'She thought it was just something built in the studio. She was thrilled when she saw it there in the main street. I had a letter from a young psychology student in England who wanted to know the price of the souvenirs. She thought it was cheaper to pay for their postage than the air fare out here to buy them.'

Strangers might not get lost in Minyip anymore. George Clark hasn't any young girl actors and their lovely legs to cheer him up. Old Herb Krause is no longer Old Codger 2. And Lofty Dugan is probably still telling the tale of his Minyip nightmare. But the locals have a reminder of the good times. Each morning the local television station plays the early episodes of *The Flying Doctors*. 'We like to watch 'em if we've got time,' said Tom Murphy. 'It's like watching old friends. We got to know some of those actors pretty well.'

And some locals might even think back to a time before television, before John Logie Baird transmitted the first flickering images, and recall a tough eccentric man of the cloth called John Flynn.

'MANTLE OF SAFETY'

One summer day in 1911, Revd John Flynn climbed to the peak of Mount Gillen, near Alice Springs, in the heart of the Australian outback. Looking across the vast, shimmering landscape, he said softly:

'One day I shall build a mantle of safety over this land.'

Today 'Flynn of the Inland's' burial ground lies at the foot of that mountain and his 'Mantle of Safety' stretches from the tip of Cape York peninsula to the far south-west corner of Western Australia, an area twice the size of Western Europe. 'The Mantle' is known as the Royal Flying Doctor Service and its founder, John Flynn, was one of the most remarkable visionaries of the twentieth century.

Obstinate, loquacious, conniving, unorthodox, exasperating and constantly at war with his seniors in the Presbyterian General Assembly, John Flynn was also a very warm human being whose foibles and eccentricities softened his towering strength and earned him something close to idolatry from the people who worked for him.

A book about *The Flying Doctors* would not be complete without an account of his extraordinary achievements. A lowly cleric, he took the emerging sciences of aviation and radio, combined them with medicine and nursing and, against impossible odds, provided safety, security, instant communication and urgent care for the people who live and travel in the five million square kilometres of the outback. In the seventy-nine years since Flynn set up his first mission, the Royal Flying Doctor Service has captured the imagination of the world and become a role model for similar services in remote regions of Africa, Asia and South America. It is part of Australia's living history. Without it, men with families would have been reluctant to pioneer the inland and the development of grazing and mineral wealth would have slowed to a snail's pace.

His optimism for Australia lay in the belief that those people who went to live in the terrifying isolation of the outback were not a bunch of crazy fools. They were the frontier men and women of Australia. Flynn firmly believed that one day, as a result of their work, the seemingly barren country would bring forth the wealth of the nation.

It is a far cry from the pedal radio to the satellite picture. It is a far cry from the primitive Halls Creek gold diggings in Northern Australia's Kimberley to the massive Roxby Downs iron ore project in South Australia. But Australia is still a frontier country and people still have to go and work and live in harsh and lonely conditions. Today, they do so under Flynn's 'Mantle of Safety'.

Like all true men of destiny, Flynn's life seemed charted from the beginning. Born in the Victorian country town of Moliagul in 1880, his family became Presbyterians because there was no Methodist Church

The Revd John Flynn, O.B.E., founder of the Royal Flying Doctor Service in 1928

nearby. But for this, it's safe to say there would be no Flying Doctor today. It was the Presbyterian Church that formed the Australian Inland Mission in 1912 and sent the newly-ordained Revd Flynn to serve in Beltana, a tiny township in South Australia's Flinders Ranges. From here he brought to life his 'impossible dream'.

Very much a hands-on man, Flynn was not simply a preacher of sermons. He could set a broken limb, was a skilled carpenter, photographer, horseman, buggy driver and strapper. Intellectually, he was a trained teacher, fluent writer, persuasive speaker, a publicist, and above all, a visionary. Opponents in the upper echelons of church power soon found they'd met their match in this 'jack-of-all-endeavours' and he was allocated funds to build a nursing home at the isolated rail link of Oodnadatta, half way between Adelaide and Alice Springs on the western edge of the Simpson Desert. It was as typical an outback town as you could find in those days, and hasn't changed much since. This is what *The Sydney Morning Herald*'s religious writer, Alan Gill, had to say about Oodnadatta in 1980 when he retraced Flynn's footsteps on the centenary of his birth:

'Flying into Oodnadatta, you can just make out the line of the "Ghan" railway below. Named after the camel train that pioneered the route last century, the railway cuts across salt pans, lakes that rarely know water, scrub and desert. As an Englishman, I felt I had arrived in the back of beyond. The plane taxied to a halt a stone's throw from Oodnadatta's pub, the grandly-named Transcontinental Hotel. Inside was like a movie set. Some Aborigines were fighting in one corner, and tough-looking outback characters in the other. Each group of drinkers surveyed me as if I were a visitor from Mars, yet there was a sign *"AIM*

Flynn, the mechanic. Flynn, the preacher was also very much a practical hands-on man

is high", on the wall. *AIM* are the initials of the Australian Inland Mission, founder of the Flying Doctor Service.

'Oodnadatta is at the front door of the Northern Territory and the back door of Queensland. In its hey-day it had three hotels, a Customs and Excise yard, Indian restaurant, cordial factory, and a Chinese market garden. It now has a school, a famous pub, cinema/communal hall, and a mission hospital with an Old Timers' annex.

'Further west, the Alice Springs Flynn Memorial Church is a fascinating building. Just outside are miniature plaques to inland heroes, many of whom, at the time the memorials were erected, were very much alive. I was particularly touched by one plaque, which bore the simple but eloquent tribute: "The best mate I ever had."'

Oodnadatta became the first link in a chain of ten other nursing homes (or hostels, as they became known) that Flynn personally designed and helped build over the next fifteen years. This network with its twenty-three nursing Sisters was part of the answer, but little use in a distant emergency. The man already dubbed as 'Flynn of the Inland' knew that two doctors served an area of 230 000 square km in Western Australia and just one supervised 800 000 square km in the Northern Territory. He had experienced the loneliness and isolation of the outback at first hand and the unrelenting fear of an accident or sudden illness with no doctor at hand.

It was the rapid development of aviation during the Great War that really stirred Flynn's imagination. By 1917, he was satisfied that aircraft (aerial ambulances) and what was then called wireless, could combine to defeat the tyranny of distance and provide health care to isolated communities. Unfortunately he was also up against the tyranny of costs. What the homesteads and outposts needed was a cheap, reliable radio transceiver simple enough to be operated by a child. It would need to be light and mobile, have a range of 500 km and cost around today's equivalent of $200. This was a tough specification at the end of the war when public broadcasting services were barely established in the cities and listeners had only 'cat's whisker' crystal receivers with headphones.

Once again fate intervened. A call came from Mt Isa (a frontier mining town in the far north-west of Queensland) for an aeroplane to bring a man suffering from a broken pelvis to hospital in Cloncurry,

Alfred Traeger, inventor of the pedal radio transceiver which enabled the first long-distance exchanges between Australia's inland people, and made the Flying Doctor Service possible. Here Traeger looks back on the days of his first pedal radio set in the early 1920s

124 km due east. Such mercy flights depended on a plane being handy at the time and were quite unofficial. As it happened, the patient was an Adelaide electrical engineer, Alfred H. Traeger, and Flynn seized the opportunity to glean from him technical advice and information. Lying in a hospital bed Traeger was unable to escape the endless flow of questions and ideas which Flynn put before him and gradually came to realise the scope and challenge of his dream. A working partnership developed between the two men and it was through Traeger's dogged persistence in designing and refining the transmitting and receiving base station that the long-awaited breakthrough came in 1928 when Traeger perfected a simple two-valve receiver operating from dry batteries. Shortly afterwards he invented the pedal generator, the basis of the pedal wireless, for use in homesteads or in the field. The 'Flying Doctor' was about to become a reality.

The first base station went into service at Cloncurry on 6 June 1929. The first pedal wireless was installed soon afterwards at August Downs station, 300 km to the north. Their first aircraft was a single-engined de Havilland chartered from Queensland and Northern Territory Aerial Services, whose initials were to become known world-wide as Australia's international airline, QANTAS. In his first year of operations, Dr K. St Vincent Welch covered 35000 km, responding to 255 calls for help, and took his flying clinic to dozens of communities without a hospital or doctor. His aircraft, *Victory*, had a flying speed of 130 km per hour. Its cramped, noisy cabin was a nightmare in the constant turbulence, high temperatures, dust and electrical storms of the outback. At the same time as he was responding to calls for help, he was dropping off pedal radios at isolated homesteads and townships. The network was building, but one problem still had to be overcome.

Low signal strength limited transmissions to Morse Code, a largely unknown skill in a land that couldn't boast the luxury of telegraph wires. Traeger eventually developed a semi-automatic Morse transmitter, a typewriter-like device with long or short slots on the arm of each key. When a key was struck, the downwards movement of the arm made a series of contacts which transmitted 'dits' or 'dahs' for each letter, ensuring error-free transmission.

Even more remarkable was Traeger's two-tone whistle, devised to activate distant radio bases after they'd been closed for the day. Shaped like the two fingers in a 'V-for-Victory' signal, the whistle was blown into the microphone for six seconds through one end, turned around and blown for four seconds through the other; producing the exact high/low frequency tone needed to activate the emergency call decoder at the base station.

For the first time, neighbours, families and friends scattered over thousands of square kilometres could exchange news and gossip on the pedal wireless. It gave the outback its 'voice'. The open discussions held each day became known as the 'galah' sessions, named after the noisy, chattering, pink and grey native parrot. From there developed the famous 'School of the Air' which replaced or supplemented correspondence courses to educate the children of the outback.

Today, the people who become flying doctors are the cornerstone of the service. Its continued success depends on their competence and dedication. They are on call day or night. Anyone with a pedal radio can be talking to the flying doctor in less time than it takes the average urban dweller to contact his local GP by telephone. Moreover, there is no place in the RFDS networks where one of their thirty-four doctors cannot reach a patient within two hours. Apart from the fourteen RFDS bases, some 3000 outposts are provided with medical chests which contain more than 100 specially selected items. Doctors prescribe drugs by referring to a number on the package, repeating it, and as further safeguard, naming it. In subsequent radio clinics the doctor will monitor the patient's progress until satisfied he or she is cured. If not satisfied, the doctor will fly out to the patient and may even order an evacuation. Last year, 12000 people were saved from life-threatening situations out of a total of 115 000 treated by the RFDS.

Their thirty-five aircraft – Beechcraft, Kingair, Conquest, Navajo and Nomad – flew 7 630 000 km. Incredibly, despite the hazards of outback landings and take-offs, by instruments in shocking weather, by hand-held flares at night, on salt pans, roads and paddocks, the RFDS won last year's Civil Aviation Authority inaugural award for the safest airline in Australia, which, given the country's matchless reputation for air safety, arguably makes the RFDS the world's safest airline!

Flynn's 'Mantle of Safety' could seek no greater plaudit.

In 1951, shortly after his death, it was proposed that the Northern Territory be re-named *Flynnland* – indeed, the real Flynnland covered more than two thirds of the continent. At the opening of the Flynn Memorial Church, Sir William Slim, the then Governor-General, said of John Flynn: 'His hands are stretched out like a benediction over the Inland. He is among the greatest Australians of this century, and perhaps the greatest Australian churchman of all time.'

The achievements stand on their own. But what about the man? According to Flynn's old friend and colleague, Revd Fred McKay:

'During his student days there were people who felt that Flynn would never make the ministry, that he was not interested enough in the traditional things to make the grade. But some people realised he had potential, gifts that were different. The sheer ambition of Flynn for his mission, particularly in the early days, was staggering.'

He had a great ability for fund-raising. This made a lasting

The children of the outback receive their lessons over the two-way radio on the 'School of Air'

impression on the six-year-old McKay when Flynn visited his home town of Walkerston, Queensland, in 1913. Flynn brought with him a wooden camel, complete with saddle packs, which he took to the children at the local Sunday school. Young McKay was so impressed that he emptied the entire contents of his money box into one of the saddle packs. Thirty-eight years later, he succeeded John Flynn as superintendent of the Australian Inland Mission and the Royal Flying Doctor Service.

Another of Flynn's ideas was an innocent piece of conniving which he delighted in calling 'The Plot'. It actually financed a survey which led to the establishment of the mission itself. In 1911 Flynn asked the Presbyterian Church to release a man to make a detailed twelve-month study of religious and medical needs 'beyond the farthest fences'. When he ran into the usual arguments over finance, he said he could raise the money out of threepences (the smallest silver coin of the time). As it was obviously another of Flynn's mad schemes, no one took any notice until he called for volunteers to help set a world record for a trail of threepenny pieces a quarter of a mile long. The publicist in Flynn had taken over. The idea caught on. People from all walks of life added their spare threepence to the trail. What no one realised was that Flynn, in his methodical way, had calculated it would take £350 worth of threepenny pieces to complete the trail and that that would be enough to finance the survey.

Flynn had no time for people who didn't share his vision. His was the typical impatience of a man of action. There were those on the board who considered him a hopeless administrator, his schemes unrealistic and someone whose mandate should not be renewed. Flynn, on the other hand, attacked the board for 'ignorance and timidity'. He complained, particularly in the early years, about the pitiable amount of money and manpower the board provided.

'After all our enthusiastic assembly declarations, publication of reports and magazines, formation of committees, campaigns in church meetings and public demonstrations, deluge of circulars and individual campaigning for funds; after all our patriotic church talk, and writing of the need for workers in Inland areas – we have increased the number of church workers in the Inland by exactly TWO MEN AND A QUARTER.'

Like all enthusiasts he was a difficult man to manage. His policy of 'venturing in faith', and, as he put it, 'choosing the path of danger', didn't appeal to the conservatism of his bosses. According to one colleague: 'He could be extremely stubborn, and the AIM board-room witnessed more than one battle of wills. To play the autocrat, however, was alien to his nature, and tensions soon subsided.'

Yet Flynn was the ideal combination of bushman and cleric, a man born to take the church's word to the lonely outback. He once said: 'The very conditions that make it difficult to get at the heart and mind of the bushman, make that heart and mind more responsive once touched.'

During his first outback journey, he ran across a shearer who told him a copy of a funeral service would have been useful when he'd buried his mate hundreds of miles from a church cemetery. All he and his companions could do was sing *Auld Lang Syne*. Flynn set up a liter-

ary fund to publish *The Bushman's Companion*, in September 1910. This small volume, described as 'just the article for pocket or saddle-bag', became something of an outback Bible. Its 111 pages included a large section on first aid, selected extracts from the Bible, hymns and prayers, a funeral service and children's service, directions for making a will, postal information, a calendar, cash account, pages for memo-randa and with a true Flynn flourish of down-to-earth realism and humour, the words of *Auld Lang Syne*.

According to Fred McKay: 'Flynn had the smell of the Bush and a feeling for people who needed security. He scarcely ever preached, he would be a hard man to get even to take a service in a home; he just wanted to talk to people.'

And Oh, could he talk!

Flynn (right) with Dr George Simpson and his wife. Simpson became the world's first Flying Doctor in 1927 when he answered an emergency call in a Qantas de Havilland 50 aircraft and brought an injured man to Cloncurry, the first Flying Doctor base

29

Apart from being a naturally talkative person, Flynn used his long-windedness as an ecclesiastical filibuster to wear down people in authority and to avoid negative answers. He would have made a super salesman. His motto was: 'Never let a person say no because tomorrow they'll probably say yes.'

He even used the technique on seasoned politicians. On a visit to Arthur Fadden, later Prime Minister, he sat on a comfortable chair, took out his pipe, and settled down for a yarn. According to Fred McKay, who was with him: 'John Flynn just sat there, lit endless matches, smoked his pipe, and talked all day. When the evening came, Fadden said, "Well, I'll have to go home," and Flynn countered, "I'll come back and see you tomorrow." We went back to our hotel and that night Fadden telephoned and said, "Don't bring John Flynn into my office again unless he has a firm proposition. I didn't know what he was talking about today." That night I said to Flynn, as tactfully as I could, "Fadden wants to help, but you'll have to come to the point." Normally a late riser, Flynn was up bright and early next morning and went straight down to Fadden's office. He was out again, beaming all over his face, in half an hour. He was a wise old cove – he'd put his proposition and he'd got the answer he wanted.

'One of his characteristics was to break off a conversation if he thought he was losing. He'd say, "Fred, have you heard this one?" and he'd tell you a rollicking bush yarn to lift the downward flow and get you listening again. He used his pipe as a distraction. He'd take it out of his pocket, put it in his mouth, and light it over and over again. All the time he was watching the other blokes, summing them up over the top of his pipe.

'It was impossible to pin him down in debate; he'd go on literally for hours, and even then you wondered whether he'd answered the questions. But he researched problems thoroughly and drew up well-formulated plans. When it came to the implementation of his dreams, he carefully selected men whom he told to "look and listen" and to go ahead as they saw best. He was a great encourager and left tasks open-ended so that his team could exercise their own faith. This is what Christ did in the New Testament.'

John Flynn's long-serving and long-suffering secretary, Jean Baird, was based in Sydney and became his informant, not to say spy, at the

heart of the church's operations. She was a good secret agent and, ever the practical man, he married her at the Presbyterian Church, Ashfield, near Sydney on 7 May 1932. Both were in middle life. The union surprised Flynn's associates, who considered him a confirmed bachelor, capable of great tenderness, but not the romantic type. He was not, in traditional terms, a good husband. Jean complained that he was a 'villain' to cook for; meals were often kept waiting for hours, and it made little difference what they were. He was well-known for his lack of punctuality. As consolation he was handy about the house, an expert at mending broken china and clocks, and when egg-beaters became scarce during World War II, he mended dozens from all over the neighbourhood.

Flynn dressed well and spent money on presents (usually going without himself). He chose his own friends and often got the wowsers in the Presbyterian Church offside. When in Sydney, he made his home in the Metropole Hotel, holding court with friends and business contacts at all hours. He was oblivious to criticism and saw no reason to leave his beloved Metropole, even after his marriage. Not only did his social habits raise eyebrows, others thought he was too un-orthodox or too 'pragmatic' in his views on theology. As he got older, opposition within the assembly became more structured. They said the mission was becoming ineffectual and Flynn was losing his grip. The gnats were nibbling at the lion.

Ten miles from Alice Springs in central Australia; the final resting place for the ashes of the Revd John Flynn

HERE REST THE ASHES OF
FLYNN OF THE INLAND

At the beginning of 1950 the board invited Fred McKay to take his place. McKay, a veteran padre and one of the most loyal of 'Flynn's Mob,' promptly told his boss. Although surprised, Flynn took it philosophically, bore no grudge and advised McKay to accept. What no one knew at the time was that the decision had already been made for them. Flynn was dying of cancer.

He'd once written: 'I can see a Cathedral of the Air at Alice Springs, with full services every Sabbath, "attended" regularly by a congregation of thousands, scattered over thousands of square miles; not to mention popular concerts several nights a week, lectures on how to get the best out of the wireless, and a daily recital of news and current events.'

Tired of the political infighting and possibly suspecting his approaching death, he returned to Alice Springs and climbed Mount Gillen to survey the reality of his dream come true. As they left, he said softly to his wife: 'This would be a lovely place to be buried.'

On 23 May 1951, a great crowd gathered at the foot of Mount Gillen to say farewell to Flynn of the Inland. The Alice Springs RFDS radio operator hit on the idea of broadcasting the service from the transmitter on the back of his truck. People from all over the outback were able to attend their hero's funeral by tuning in on their pedal radios.

The 'Mantle of Safety' was paying its last tribute.

BEGINNINGS

With the death of Flynn, it seemed that the romantic heart had been plucked from the Royal Flying Doctor Service. Scriptwriter Terry Stapleton certainly thought so. His research in Melbourne had revealed a highly efficient, nationwide airborne medical service that seemed, on the surface, to be light years from the old image of cowboy pilots and death-defying doctors. At least that was the mental picture he had on the afternoon he stepped from his air-conditioned Fokker aircraft into the heat and dust and flies of Charleville Airport. It was 110 degrees in the shade – if you could find any – and he wondered for the millionth time what the hell he was doing there. A former actor from genteel, temperate Adelaide, he needed the searing outback like a moth needed an insect zapper. His mission was to research the possibilities of a television mini-series on the Royal Flying Doctor Service (RFDS) but at the moment he felt more like a write-off than a writer. Things weren't about to improve.

At the baking airport terminal he was approached by a man in shirt sleeves, shorts and elastic-sided boots.

'G'day,' he said. 'You must be the television bloke.'

'How do you do,' said Stapleton, taking his extended hand. 'Dr Kendall, I presume.'

The man grunted, not at all amused, picked up Stapleton's suitcase and led the way into the world's dirtiest station-wagon, a battered Ford coated in thick red dust from the bottom of the tyres to the top of the aerial. There was assorted junk and a garbage can in the back. They pulled up outside a run-down pub he'd been warned about by his boss at Crawford Productions in Melbourne. Dismayed, Stapleton said:

'I thought I'd been booked into the Charleville Hotel.'

Kendall ignored him and strode off to the reception office, which was as wide open and empty as the streets outside, and started fumbling about for keys. Stapleton waited, worried, dodged flies and

The flying doctor service

stepped around dried vomit on the verandah.

'No one around,' said Kendall, emerging from the front door. 'Wait on, I'll try the office.'

Stapleton followed him inside. The office was empty too but they found his name in the register and a note saying: 'Key to room 6 in door.' By now Stapleton had a pretty good idea that one thing he didn't have to worry about in Charleville was somebody breaking into his room. It was small consolation. The room itself was entirely without cheer or comfort. There was a television but no fridge. The television didn't work. Outside it was still 110 degrees. Kendall said:

'You'll be sweet now until tomorrow, right?'

Stapleton had fondly imagined he'd be invited home for a meal or even a few drinks and a talk about the project in air-conditioned comfort. Not so. Kendall zoomed off in his station-wagon and that just left Stapleton and the flies and it was only 2.45 p.m. on a Sunday afternoon.

Outside it was still 110 degrees.

(opposite) A Flying Doctor display showing the doctor's radio and basic medicines. The medicine bottles are numbered enabling the doctor to prescribe drugs over the air more simply and safely for isolated patients not in need of immediate attention

Originator, researcher and scriptwriter for the series, Terry Stapleton

Time passed like a crippled snail. He went for a walk down the wide dusty street trying to soak up the atmosphere. A young bloke in a wide brimmed hat tapped him on the shoulder and asked the way to Morven. When Stapleton said he didn't know, the young bloke looked at him angrily.

'What are you, one of those bloody tourists?'

The town was plainly a dead loss. He went back to the pub. There was a sign saying *Join us for the time of your life* and another saying *Dining Room*. The dining room wasn't open on Sundays and there wasn't any sign of 'us', or indeed, the time of his life. He went out wandering again and eventually discovered the only place open was a Chinese restaurant. In outback Charleville. Not only that, the food was genuine Chinese and quite tasty. He headed back to his room, puzzled but sleepy. It wasn't 110 degrees anymore, only a mere 105.

He was just dozing off when there came the loud roar of a motor outside, a screech of brakes, doors slamming and footsteps thundering down the hall. He jerked upright, staring in horror as more cars pulled up, doors slammed endlessly, engines revved, horns blared, and the weatherboard pub with its paper thin walls shook to an invading horde. The room next to Stapleton's was inhabited by telephone linesmen and the local shearers, riggers, drovers, cockies and rouseabouts had arrived for the standard Sunday night rage. Soon the music was blaring, drunks singing, girls screaming, everyone roaring with laughter and a great time was being had by all – except the lone occupant of the room next door.

At one stage he thought of going out to tell them to shut up, but a peek through the curtains as they lumbered past with cartons of beer on their shoulders swiftly dispelled such heroic ambitions. As he said later, 'They were all built like oil tankers.' So he lay on the bed, wondering what monstrous past transgressions he was atoning for.

'I'd never wanted to do the thing in the first place. My boss, the late Hector Crawford, used to come up with four ideas every ten minutes and when he suggested a series on the Flying Doctor I thought it sounded about as exciting as a series on the Red Cross. Very worthy and all that, but how do you make it work? Anyhow, he kept on and on at me and eventually, to shut him up, I agreed to go to the Flying Doctor base at Charleville and have a poke around.'

Hollow-eyed and dead on his feet at 9 a.m., Terry went out to the RFDS base to meet the airborne saviours of the outback. That's when he got the bad news. Flying Doctor Kendall McLelland explained that the old days no longer existed. Flying planes stuck together by chewing gum through tropical cyclones and landing on boggy outback cow paddocks to whisk the dying shearers from the jaws of death – those sort of things were from the legendary past. Today's Flying Doctor, said McLelland, was little more than a mobile GP. With faster, safer aircraft, earlier diagnosis and preventative drugs there were few emergencies and little drama. Stapleton realised if he was going to get anything out of the trip it would have to be on personalities. He was yet to discover that Kendall, like most outback Australians, was somewhat prone to understatement. What he took for granted, city dwellers like Stapleton found not only astonishing, but bloody frightening.

In passing, McLelland told the story of an accident at the Birdsville Races, Australia's most celebrated bush race meeting and the outback equivalent to the English Derby or the Melbourne Cup. Farmers,

(above left) 1940s Flying Doctor, Dr Russell Jones hurries through a dust storm to his patient. Such storms have been one of the service's chief hazards as poor visibility hinders location of airstrips

(above right) Dr Jones with his son at Broken Hill airport, the headquarters of the service

shearers, people from all over the north travelled literally thousands of miles to watch the horses ploughing up the clouds of red dust. Even the city newspapers carried form guides and results. It also happened to be an RFDS fund-raising event and the Flying Doctor always parked nearby, not just to show the flag, but also to deal with any emergencies such as a fall, as well as inevitable cuts, bruises, broken limbs and abrasions from spectators getting drunk and beating each other up. Having a good time in the outback often equates to inflicting as much physical damage on somebody as he inflicts on you – often quite a lot.

A drunk had fallen off the back of a truck, was bleeding from the nose and the ears and sinking into a coma. Kendall suspected an emergency operation to relieve the pressure on the patient's brain was needed, but they were three hours from the nearest hospital. During the flight, to confirm his diagnosis, Kendall radioed the specialist at Charleville Hospital. He received confirmation that the emergency operation, known as a craniotomy, was needed. Kendall didn't have any proper instruments on the flight so he started digging into the drunk's head with a pair of scissors. By the time they got to Charleville the inside of the aircraft looked like an abattoir but the drunk survived and is doubtless still knocking back OP (over proof) rum and schooners in some outback pub.

Hearing this, Stapleton began to see the possibilities for drama that lay beneath the easy banter of RFDS staff and he decided to go on a flight to see if the Flying Doctor really was just a 'mobile GP'. Australia's most successful outback television drama was about to be born – but not without considerable trauma for the midwife.

What follows has been gleaned from Stapleton's notes on the trip, and shows the scriptwriter's meticulous eye for detail, sense of atmosphere and deft dramatic touch. Much of what he saw that day was later plotted into the series and served to establish a sense of realism and authenticity which earned the grudging approval of viewers in the outback who were not an easy bunch to please and at first thought the chances of some flash city cove getting it right were on a par with the Flying Doctor getting around in a seaplane.

Kendall picked up Stapleton at 7.15 a.m. on Tuesday morning to go to the airport. By then he'd transferred to a room on the other side of the pub, but had still woken at 4.00 a.m., full of nameless apprehensions. They called at a bakery on the way and Kendall collected several loaves of fresh bread which the RFDS distributed at their various ports of call along the clinic run. It struck Stapleton as being rather biblical. Manna from Heaven? At the airport they met Bill, the pilot, striding briskly around dressed in a white short-sleeved shirt with epaulettes, brown slacks, black shoes and wearing a tie. This was standard RFDS pilot gear (tie optional). The Sister was Dianne Briscoe, a rather homely, bespectacled woman of about thirty. Blue hat, red jacket, blue skirt. She greeted him with total disinterest and continued to roll a cigarette.

They loaded up the Beechcraft with the doctor's and sister's cases and Bill told him where to sit and what to do in an emergency. Everyone settled down and the assistant engineer, Bob, called out from the ground 'See you tomorrer night – hopefully.' Bill gave him the traditional thumbs-up and off they went. Stapleton asked Bill the differences between the Beechcraft and the Nomad. He snorted with contempt. 'The Nomad's a terrible aircraft. The tails are always falling off and everything. If you see a Nomad overhead you better go and hide under something.' That seemed to take care of Nomads.

After a fifty minute flight they approached Yaraka airstrip. It looked very rough to Stapleton but Bill said it was just fine, although it 'went out' very quickly after rain. Ten points would see them stranded. Stapleton looked anxiously at the cloudy sky. As they touched down, a wild black pig ran across their path and darted into the bush. If they'd connected with it, the results would have been catastrophic. No one seemed to notice. The plane bounced and jarred its way over what seemed like a ploughed field. Bill yawned as they drew to a halt. Stapleton shook his head, realising once again that what was 'just fine' for them would have the passengers on a normal scheduled flight wide-eyed with terror.

They set up business in a room at the back of Yaraka Hall. By then an informal queue had developed, mainly youngish mothers and their children, one drover type in a stetson, and one ninety-two-year-old bloke in a black coat, a shirt without a collar, cowboy boots and a clear burnished complexion. A spaniel dozed in the queue and the kids rampaged around the hall while Sister Dianne set up in one corner and dealt with the mothers and babies. They all knew her. She weighed the babies, administered injections, gossiped with them and rolled ciga-rettes. Cattle browsed outside. Across the road was a tiny, deserted rail-way station with a few 'Wanted for Murder' posters stuck to the wall. Near the station were two depressing looking houses with kids playing noisily and aimlessly outside in wrecked cars and goods wagons with grass growing between the spokes of their wheels.

Back in the hall, he joined Jan and Evelyn as they completed the washing-up after morning tea. Jan and her husband owned a station; Evelyn and her husband managed one. Both women complained

A Flying Doctor administers to an injured patient in the stark conditions of the outback

cheerfully of the never-ending domestic chores. They cooked not only for their families but also for the ringers, shearers and rouseabouts. The women said that no sooner had they washed up after breakfast then it was time for smoko.* Then lunch, afternoon tea and dinner. Both women explained how they took a while to adjust to city life when they were on holidays. They had become so used to speaking loudly, it was very hard to remember to modify their voices in a motel room. And harder for the kids.

Jan's daughter was an entrant in the annual RFDS 'Queen of the Outback' beauty contest. (Stapleton seized on that as the title and theme of an early episode.) He asked to use the toilet and Evelyn directed him outside and laughingly said she hoped there'd be no snakes or frogs. When he flushed the toilet a small, startled frog emerged from the swirling water and began a life or death struggle, clawing its way up the bowl. It survived. So life mooched on in Yaraka.

After lunch, the local cop drove them frantically back to the airstrip. Stapleton gripped the edges of his seat and tried to press his feet through the floor as Bill, the pilot, explained the most dangerous parts of a Flying Doctor's life were the drives to and from the airstrips. They took off and Bill invited him to sit in the co-pilot's seat. Stapleton knew then he'd been accepted.

They put in briefly at a tiny township named Stonehenge (Stapleton never discovered why) and headed for Jundah, the overnight stop. There they were met by Gordon McLeod in a Landrover. Gordon immediately began a happy stream of abuse, sending up Bill for wearing a tie and being late. Kendall introduced Stapleton as Terry Shakespeare – not because he was being half-smart, Kendall confessed later, he'd just forgotten his name. Asked about his recent holiday, Gordon said: 'Don't bloody talk to me about holidays. The first day we were away Jason got bitten by a snake and bloody died. The second day Bruce caught the flu and never stopped coughin' and spewin'. It was all downhill after that. What else do y'wanna know?' Immune as he was becoming to their casual attitude to life, Stapleton was horrified at their equally casual disdain of death – until he learnt Jason was a pet donkey.

---

* smoko: slang term for a cigarette break.

Gordon MacLeod told him that where you have goannas you don't have snakes. He once had two pet goannas called Charlie and Tuesday. One had come to the back porch and begged for food and used to stop the lawn sprinkler long enough to stand under it and have a shower.

'Used to live under the old hospital but it burnt down when they were away hibernating so they shot through,' said Gordon. 'Where you been anyhow? I got sick a waitin' for y'z and went down the bloody pub. That ear-pickin'-up bludger was up to his tricks again. He reckons I done the wrong thing. I was talkin' to Clive for a minute and all of a sudden bloody Happy –'

'Who's Happy?'

'He's the bloody ear-pickin'-up bludger I was talkin' about.'

'What's an ear-picking-up . . .'

'He picks you up by the ears. You pick a bloke up by the ears and he's powerless. His hands go straight to his ears, because of the bloody pain.'

'I see.'

'Anyrate, bloody Happy turned me around and said "Not bloody good enough to talk to, aren't I?" But I quietened him down. He thinks he's got me bluffed, but he hasn't.'

This all seemed a little bewildering, but everyone else took it in their stride, so Stapleton decided not to probe further. Then there was a roar and a screech and a utility truck swirled to a halt. The very same Happy Matthews had arrived.

He strode into the bar. The forewarning had not been exaggerated. He was about six feet and twenty-four stone. A girth beyond belief. It preceded him to the bar, bursting out of his shirt. He wore shorts, the obligatory cowboy hat, and no shoes. He was carrying a huge, freshly caught fish which he slapped down on the bar and then yelled for a drink. To Stapleton it was like an overweight John Wayne striding into the saloon in Dodge City.

Kendall said Happy had been to see him some time ago, hoping for some miracle cure for his obesity. Kendall had told him the bleak facts of life: that there was no miracle cure or tablet. The only hope was a strict regimen of diet and exercise and curtailed drinking and smoking, otherwise Happy would be dead within five years. Kendall said that not only did Happy ignore all the advice but now regarded

Kendall as a thorough bastard who wanted to fit him out for a wooden suit. Happy seemed to have the whole town terrorised. Stapleton mentally jotted down another episode.

The next morning it was pouring with rain and Stapleton grimly recalled Bill's warning that ten points would see them stuck on the ground. He didn't fancy a long stay in Jundah, especially if Happy took it into his head to seek a new set of ears. At the airport he learnt they were flying to Windorah to refuel in case they had to circle Charleville and wait for the weather to clear. It wasn't a very promising start to the day, and by the time they were airborne it was a lot worse, the Beechcraft being hurled around by turbulence. The rain and storms lasted all the way to Windorah. They'd no sooner landed than it was time to take off for Eromanga where they'd only had three points. On the way they thought they'd 'drop into' Plevna Downs station for lunch. The trip was supposed to take twenty minutes, but after forty minutes in the air and judging from the animated conversation and map checking between Kendall and Bill, it was clear they were lost. Feeling a little out of place, Stapleton asked Dianne. She rolled another cigarette and stared into the rain lashing at their windows.

'Pilots never get lost,' she said casually. 'Sometimes there's a temporary disorientation.'

They eventually found the station and put down for lunch before taking off for Eromanga and Windorah. They hit a full-blown electrical storm and once again the tiny Beechcraft was thrown all over the place. This time even the RFDS crew were eyeing the sky with trepidation and for someone with Stapleton's limited experience of small aircraft, the flight was nothing short of terrifying. Once again they'd lost their way and the turbulence was so bad Bill decided to put down at the first airstrip they came to.

Stapleton was getting a firsthand display of genuine heroism, of which they were totally unaware. It was all in a day's work, these hair-raising landings when they didn't know if they were heading into a bog or hard ground, flying hundreds of miles through appalling weather to mend broken limbs and sometimes broken minds. They were almost hero-worshipped by the people of the outback. They might dismiss the myth of the old Flying Doctor, but as far as Stapleton was concerned, he lived on – with a vengeance!

A Nomad N22B aircraft, not very highly recommended by Bill, the pilot who flies Stapleton on his first air trip with the service

Quite unconsciously, Kendall in his wide-brimmed hat, easy approach, matter-of-fact authority, dry humour and confidence in an emergency, presented the perfect television image of the Flying Doctor. Stapleton was sure that if they could capture and dramatise the reality of the man they couldn't miss. Then there was the nurse in her colourful uniform being plonked down on some rough airstrip east of nowhere, rammed into an uncomfortable car and rushed into a sweltering small town to cure the sick, mend the injured and maybe save a few lives. Once again, they took it for granted and didn't see the drama or incredibility of the image. At one stage they went into a skid at 60 m.p.h. on a dirt road and lost control, careered about hitting rocks and almost turned over. After a short silence everybody started making jokes about the number of times that sort of thing had happened. As far as Stapleton was concerned it was a genuine brush with death.

During the flight to Charleville the rain increased, the visibility was almost zero and Kendall said they'd have to do an instrument landing. This was an exercise Bill practised at least every six months with the supervision of the Chief Test Pilot in Brisbane. He was either blindfolded or a shade was put over his instrument panel and had to take off and land the aircraft blind. Provided everything went right, you didn't see or feel a thing until you were actually on the strip. A small error, Kendall helpfully explained, meant you touched down nose first.

Now, with the aircraft being tossed around the blackening sky like a fly in a fan, Stapleton hanging on like grim death and Bill desperately trying to radio Charleville through the barrage of static, Kendall casually suggested they hatch up some plots for the television series. Stapleton stared at him, wondering if he'd heard correctly. But there was method in Kendall's madness. When Stapleton finally collected his wits and got involved in what he knew best, scripting, he became so preoccupied that he didn't have a lot of time to surrender to mind-boggling terror.

Approaching Charleville they learnt there was another aircraft in the area. Kendall helpfully explained again that this would increase the danger of a mid-air collision in all the rain and cloud. They eventually touched down safely and for the first time since his arrival, the noisy old pub looked like a welcome home. Stapleton had a very large beer. He was still at the bar when the evening news came on. Up came the weather maps showing cloud almost blanketing Queensland. There was spontaneous cheering and applause from the bar but it didn't last long. Farmers are not a happy lot. After such unseemly jubilation, they started worrying about the inevitable cold snap and whether frost would wipe out the new vegetation.

On his return to Melbourne, Terry Stapleton was very excited about the trip and after a long talk with Hector Crawford, they decided on a six hour mini-series. One of Australia's best scriptwriters, Stapleton (now fifty-seven) insisted on sticking to real events as the backbone of the plots. Before leaving Charleville, he'd had a long talk with Dr Kendall's predecessor, Dr Timothy O'Leary. After twenty-five years in the RFDS, he'd become a legend in the outback and Crawfords brought him to Melbourne and picked his brain for anecdotes and plot outlines. In the mini-series he was to become Dr Harry Sinclair, about to reluctantly hang up his stethoscope in favour of the young Dr Tom Callaghan, loosely based on Dr Kendall.

It did so well in the ratings that the Nine Network agreed to go along with a series. Even then, they still didn't realise what a winner they'd stumbled on. Crawford's Chief Executive Officer, Terry Ohlsson, said:

'Now that we're completing our eighth series, we're beginning to realise "Doctors" could last forever. The ingredients are magic: the great outdoors, medicine, loneliness, drama, heroism, romance, mystery, adventure, the difficulties of communication and central characters who fly around in planes and can be placed anywhere you like without affecting the authenticity. It's perhaps the best mix for a continuing drama series ever devised.'

Ohlsson insisted *The Flying Doctors* was not a soapie. He likened it more to a series of one act plays that could be broadcast in or out of sequence. It was the only film-originated series being made in Australia and demanded the very best of its scriptwriters. This could explain its appeal overseas, although, as Stapleton pointed out, *Neighbours* was very big in Europe and there was no way they could pull a scriptwriter from *Neighbours* to do one of their storylines. What, then, was its European appeal? Stapleton explains:

'Well, for a start, you've got doctors who fly around in aeroplanes to see their patients. That's pretty exotic stuff in a place as urbanised as Europe, with the cities so close together. Then there's the doctor/ patient relationship. It's the equivalent to flying from Amsterdam to Brussels to put someone's arm in a splint. Imagine how that appeals to people who are just numbers queuing up in some National Health clinic.

'Then there's the hot climate, open skies compared to smog, an emptiness and the chance of being isolated which is becoming almost impossible to find south of Greenland. But probably the most important thing, both here and overseas, are the wholesome values of the show. I can leave my seven-year-old kid to watch it without any qualms. There's a lot of alleged family programmes where I wouldn't do that. People want those old values back again. We know that from the tremendous amount of mail we get from Europe. We don't swear, we avoid distasteful, sensational subjects. That's not to say we won't tackle something like AIDS or abuse of aborigines. But we're not here to make some great moral point. We're to provide wholesome, family entertainment. We've been there longer than *Neighbours* and our audience is still growing. In a sense we blazed Australia's trail into the family viewing market in Europe. Of all the Australian series sold overseas, *The Flying Doctors* is the best.'

THE FLYING DOCTOR

Take one!

The scene called for some innocent love-play in the waters of the Coopers Creek billabong. Flying Doctor Tom Callaghan (Andrew McFarlane) was having a mild fling with Dr Chris Randall (Liz Burch). As they drifted closer, gazing deeply into each other's eyes, the camera zoomed in for the clinch. It was a beautiful, tender moment. Then Liz shrieked:

'Stop that Andrew!' She slapped his face and started thrashing around in the water.

McFarlane stared. The film crew stared. This wasn't in the script.

'Stop what?' demanded Australia's leading television heart-throb.

'Pinching my bottom – Ow! There! You did it again!' Her voice faltered. McFarlane was a long, rangy bloke, but he'd have needed rubber arms to reach her from that distance. 'If it's not you. . .' her voice trailed off.

'Ooh!' yelled Andrew. 'Something's biting me!'

On the bank, the director was too dumbfounded to yell 'Cut!' in traditional style as everyone stared at the two love-birds floundering and bawling at each other in the billabong. Then Liz bore aloft a small, green-brown creature.

'Yabbies!' screamed Liz. 'They're eating me alive!'

Screaming and choking alternately, she struck out for the shore, closely followed by her pop-eyed Flying Doctor hero, while the crew fell about laughing. Yabbies, the small freshwater crayfish which inhabit Australia's inland lakes and dams, had brought down the Flying Doctors' romantic scene with a splash!

'Not only were we being eaten alive, the water was absolutely freezing,' Andrew recalled later. 'Liz hates being cold. She loathes it so much it makes her feel really crabby. Perhaps yabbie would be a better word. They actually have it all on film but had to cut most of it because of the language. I saw an out-take of the stuff that didn't go to air and it was very, very funny.'

Gentle romance had become high comedy.

Take two!

Deborah Kerr was whispering. As Andrew McFarlane approached the great English actress on the stage of Melbourne's Comedy Club, he could barely hear a word she was saying. Neither could the audience. He had no choice but to whisper back. Then the method behind Deborah Kerr's madness became apparent. Two people in the front row had been talking loudly. As Deborah's voice lowered, so did theirs. Soon they were silent, craning forward to catch the words on stage. Deborah stared straight at them and suddenly raised her voice to full, theatrical gusto. The guilty parties bounced back in their seats and remained silent for the rest of the performance. They'd got the message.

(below right) Andrew McFarlane, the first Flying Doctor in the series, Dr Tom Callaghan

'Really great mates' – relaxing off-screen, Liz Burch and Andrew McFarlane

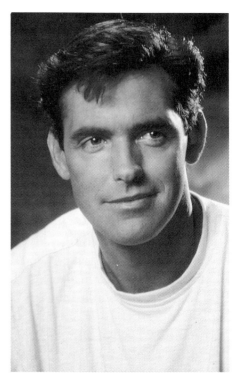

It was one of the many tricks of the trade Andrew learnt from the famous star of stage and screen. That role as the fast-talking lawyer in *The Day After the Fair* raised him to the top bracket of Australian actors. Shortly afterwards he returned to the highly popular *The Sullivans* and then the ABC television series *Patrol Boat* and eventually *The Flying Doctors*. Today, an autographed picture signed, 'To darling Andrew, all my affection and love always. Deborah Kerr' sits on an oak sideboard in Andrew's dining room to remind him of the day glib comedy became masterful technique.

In many ways these two stories mirror the dual personality of Andrew McFarlane. A classic gemini (he was born on 1 June 1941) he bears all the characteristics of his star sign as outlined by famous astrologer Marie-Simone. On the one hand he is charming and outgoing and on the other inquisitive, withdrawn and intellectual – his moods as changeable as the weather. Sometimes shy, sometimes outspoken, he shares the twin personality syndrome so common in actors such as world-renowned geminis Sir Laurence Olivier, whose formal, withdrawn manner concealed a playful, boyish nature, and Marilyn Monroe, whose coquettish charm concealed a deeply troubled individual.

Among Australia's top male leads, McFarlane is regarded as one of the best. He uses an understated style of screen acting. He communicates through facial expressions rather than words. He works assiduously at his trade and takes it very seriously.

'I do like fully understanding a role, then playing it from deep within. Maybe sometimes I get it so understated it becomes a blur,' said McFarlane, his own toughest critic. 'You can't hide mistakes. Something happens when you are doing film. The camera is rolling and pointing at you, and it draws something from within. It's like some kind of electrical charge going through you and you really feel yourself being sucked into the lens. There is a saying "That the camera steals your soul". I try to get to the soul of the character I'm playing.'

His perception of Dr Tom Callaghan is complete, but played at the surface.

'He's a well-rounded character. He makes mistakes. He's impatient and he gets frustrated and he hates being in the outback. He's not that sympathetic to begin with, although I think I could have played him more anti-sympathetic. I probably should have. But basically it's an outback love story with a bit of adventure thrown in. It's good, solid, middle-of-the-road family entertainment.'

Andrew doesn't hate the outback, but he once told critic Andrew Brock he wasn't all that fond of the surrogate outback of the television series.

'I hate early rising, but we have to get up at 5 a.m. and then stand in the freezing cold and frost in shirt-sleeves and pretend we're having a good time in the outback while some sadist sprays you with water and then turns it to ice with a wind machine.' He sighed. 'But I suppose everything has a good side. Because we're all maniacs on *The Flying Doctors* they whip maximum performance from us. On most productions, you get to shoot about four minutes a day of usable footage. We do nine and ten minutes. We've almost got to like it. There's a terrible sado-masochistic element in actors, and unfortunately producers and directors know it . . . and prey on it!'

Andrew in an episode from the series, 'A Good Drop of Red'

Andrew McFarlane's theatrical roots run deep. While on a promotional tour of the USA, he visited relatives in New Hampshire who are very special descendants of Andrew's great uncle – a man he never knew but whose framed sepia photograph has hung on his bedroom wall since he was a child. 'He is a sort of family legend if you like. I've been hearing stories about him ever since I can remember. He went off to London in the early 1900s, played in Galsworthy plays, then went to Hollywood and was part of the Golden Age. He was a character actor. He did those incredible old movies like *The Bride of Frankenstein*, *The Count of Monte Cristo*, *Anne of Green Gables* and *Smilin' Through* with Norma Shearer. His name was O.P. Heggie and you see his credits at the end of those old movies they show on late night television. His daughters in America have trunks full of letters from people like George Bernard Shaw.'

The Sullivans, a saga set in World War II, was Andrew's first major role. *The Sullivans* was also the first Australian drama series – don't dare call it a soapie – which made a favourable impression on overseas viewers.

Andrew played John Sullivan, a do-gooder and a little boring perhaps, but a good chap. 'He was a bit of a Voltaire,' said Andrew. 'He was admirable in that sense, but I thought he was a bit of a drip at times, really. I wanted him to have balls, but whenever I said that to the directors and writers, they threw a woman at me. They thought, "Oh, he needs to get his rocks off. That'll calm him down." That wasn't what I meant at all.'

After a while, he decided he was tired of John Sullivan, or as he described it: 'You can only stay in bed with one person for so long. Otherwise you get bored. You've got to get up and have breakfast sometime.'

The producers of *The Sullivans* thought he was mad. He was leaving a successful show at a time when actors were spending more time in dole queues than in front of the cameras.

'What are you going to do?' they asked.

'I don't know,' he said. And he didn't but held firmly to his theory that an actor needed to be out of work to get work. Around this time he made a movie called *Break of Day*, an interesting project in that most of it was filmed around dawn, giving it a soft, gentle glow. It meant also that even pub scenes were filmed at an hour when the body would rather be doing something sensible, like sleeping. The filming for the pub scene began at 6 a.m. 'I am meant to be drunk in it so I started drinking white wine at 5 a.m. after getting to bed at 3 a.m.' Andrew still speaks of it with a feeling akin to horror. 'By the time we broke for lunch at midday they found me asleep in a drain outside the pub.'

Then along came *Patrol Boat*, a series based on the small naval ships that patrol Australia's vast and isolated northern coastline looking for drug-runners, bird-smugglers, illegal migrants and foreign invaders. *Patrol Boat* was also moderately successful overseas.

His character was similar to John Sullivan, another reliable, safe person who never did anything wrong, the sort of image the Royal Australian Navy would like to use in its recruiting campaigns. 'It's hard to play against type unless you have a very malleable face, but I try and steer myself away and push myself into other areas if I can.'

After *Patrol Boat* he worked here and there before taking on the role

Andrew played another Tom in the film, *Break of Day*, a bittersweet love story set during World War I

of Dr Tom Callaghan in *The Flying Doctors*. Dr Tom was a bit of a do-gooder as well, reliable and safe, but Andrew saw potential beyond this characterisation. 'He's impatient and he gets frustrated and he hates the place. He hates being in the outback. He's not that sympathetic to begin with.'

At the beginning *The Flying Doctors* was to be no more than a mini-series. Much of it was filmed far from the easily accessible Minyip, out in the dustier parts of New South Wales, out where the legends were born. 'It wasn't the easiest country to work in because it's hot and it's dry and because of the distances we had to travel. We filmed in a lot of the areas used in the *Mad Max* movies. It's very stark but it has got its own kind of hypnotic beauty . . .'

Viewers liked the mini-series. The critics were kind. Crawford Productions and the Nine Network, which screened the mini-series, took the plunge and went into an expensive series. Andrew stayed around for a while but soon the restlessness within him, the dislike of spend-

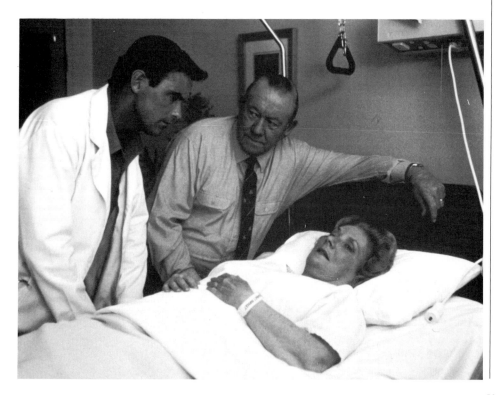

Andrew in 'Dangerous Games' with Maurie Fields and Val Jallay as Vic and Nancy Buckley

ing too long in one show, overcame the security of a regular pay packet. 'I need to get some dirt on my face,' he announced. 'I need some life experience.'

Andrew departed for the culture and excitement of London. Dr Tom departed for the famine and disease of Eritrea.

For a year he lived in London, not working, just absorbing the atmosphere of the city, which he was able to afford to do thanks to a toothpaste commercial. When he returned to Australia he got roles in television series, a telemovie, *Barracuda*, a feature movie, *Boulevard of Broken Dreams*, and on the stage.

At the same time Alan Bateman, an experienced producer who had devised, among others, the soapie, *Home and Away*, had taken over as head of drama for the Nine Network. The ratings for *The Flying Doctors* had been a little disappointing; Bateman believed all it needed was revamping. Andrew McFarlane and Dr Tom Callaghan could be the answer. He thought how sensible it was sending Dr Tom to Eritrea and

The much-admired Andrew McFarlane

not killing him off in a plane crash or with snakebite. Over a pleasant Italian meal, Andrew agreed it would be nice to return. The deal was done. Dr Tom returned to Coopers Crossing. 'I was away long enough to forget all the lousy location shoots in freezing weather,' said Andrew.

When he walked on to the set again after his absence, one of the hands asked: 'Is it good to be back?'

'Yes, it's really nice, actually,' Andrew replied.

'Oh, it must have been traumatic, though?'

'What do you mean?' said Andrew, puzzled. 'Working with all these people again? Having to sign the contract?'

'No, when you were over there, seeing all that?'

The hand, even though he was working on the set, had become as confused as many viewers had. He thought Andrew had been to Eritrea along with Dr Tom.

The break changed Andrew, as it did his character. 'Dr Tom is quite different in that he's disillusioned,' Andrew told the *Sunday Telegraph*. 'One of the strengths before was that he always saw the other side of things; he was always helping other people. Even when he had problems he knew that he had one and he'd take himself up. He was a good and caring doctor. But this time it's deeper than that. It's not a big fuss. Maybe he'll go back there – he doesn't know – but he just had to get away from it. It was too much to handle . . . the corruption of it all.'

And Andrew? Had he changed?

'I've had some really interesting experiences, personal as well as professional, so they change you. You just grow. It's a bit like putting on weight or losing weight. You stay the same person but there are certain changes within you. It's changed me in the sense that when I came back from England I had a much more positive attitude to my work. I was willing to take a lot more chances in things. I wasn't as inhibited as I used to be . . . I was prepared to take certain risks and make a fool of myself. The trap with television series is that you can fall back on mannerisms and habits and you're not really progressing, you're consolidating, you're not growing. I think you have to do that as an actor. That's why I put myself out of work at times, too, because I think you're only going to get work and new opportunities if you're out of work.'

THE NEW FLYING DOCTOR

The producers had a problem. Who on earth could they get to replace Andrew McFarlane, the lanky, easy-going actor about to take wings after two years setting his stamp firmly on the lead role in *The Flying Doctors*. Casting agents were consulted. Actors auditioned. Talent scouts unleashed. But no one, it seemed, could project the exact mixture of easy intelligence, laconic humour and tall, bronzed Aussie good looks integral to the part.

Then someone had a brainwave. If they couldn't join 'em, why not beat 'em? Get someone who was the complete opposite, introduce him towards the end of that year's series, get him established and then let the fans confront the same dilemma as the producers when Andrew makes his shock announcement. Hopefully they'd come to terms with the fact that there was only one Andrew McFarlane and copycats were out of the question.

And what was the opposite to a dedicated country doctor? An alcoholic city doctor, of course!

Daring by any standards, the ploy worked, mainly because no one bothered to tell Robert Grubb, the new Flying Doctor, just exactly what they were up to!

When he auditioned, Robert thought his role was that of a third doctor with Andrew McFarlane and Liz Burch still sharing the leads. At that stage he'd never even seen the show. They called him in for an audition and, as far as he knew, it was just a story about a community in a small town. A little bit like *A Country Practice* in the outback. When he read the script he realised it was about a doctor who wrongly diagnoses his wife. She dies of cancer and he hits the bottle out of guilt.

'I thought, wow!' Robert said later. 'They're really stretching the parameters here. Doctor leaves city after death of wife, becomes alcoholic in country town. The tyranny of guilt matched by the tyranny of distance. It has great Chekhovian qualities.'

A graduate from the National Institute of Dramatic Art, Robert naturally wanted to play Hamlet, and this looked about as close to high drama as he was ever going to get on the small screen. It wasn't until rehearsals that he discovered they were actually looking for someone who they hoped would develop into a hero to replace Andrew, but by then he'd put so much into developing the anti-hero that it was too late to change.

'So there we were, me playing the role of the city slicker alcoholic doctor right to the hilt and being told, at the last minute, that in the next episode he quits the drink and that's that.

'I thought, wait a minute, what happened to my Chekhovian character? And they said, well, we can't have a guilt-ridden doctor getting sloshed in front of the kids at 7.30 p.m. at night. He reforms, that's what happens. Bang goes the character I'd spent weeks perfecting.

'I ended up compromising. Because he was from the city, I made him very different, even to wearing expensive suits, silk shirts and Italian shoes. Andrew always wore moleskins and short sleeves and that sort of thing. I felt it was a good contrast with plenty of potential.

'Anyhow, it came off. As the character developed I was slowly accepted by the townspeople even though I'd scoot around in a Porsche wearing sunglasses and looking like something out of *Miami Vice*. We got a lot of comedy value out of it. It's always good to know the unpopular fellow is going to be caught out. You play it to the hilt at the start so he has further to drop.

'Ironically, three months later I had a break and went to Adelaide to do the stage production of *Wild Honey* and there was this marvellous part of a doctor who hits the bottle and keeps saying wonderful things like: "I love people. I just can't stand sick people. They make me depressed."'

Robert roared with laughter as he told the tale.

An extremely talented actor, Robert made the role very much his own. He has a good feel for outdoor action with juicy parts in *Mad Max Beyond Thunderdome*, *Gallipoli*, *Phar Lap*, *Robbery Under Arms*, *Sarah Dane* and *Five Mile Creek* (with new co-star Liz Burch).

'*The Flying Doctors* is very real. The episodes are based on actual

Robert Grubb (far left) in the film *Gallipoli*

events. I told a funny story about Sam Neill when we were making *Robbery Under Arms* and they leapt on it and turned it into a subplot for one of the episodes.'

The story is worth repeating, not only because it's very funny but also because it gives an insight into the genesis of film scripts. This one came from a camp-fire chat while the team was shooting way out beyond Minyip, but it could just as easily have been a couple of paragraphs from a newspaper, something overheard in a bar, a passing comment from a cab driver, something the neighbour said to the scriptwriter's wife, or even, on occasion, history itself.

Robbery Under Arms was being shot in the scorching outback heat beyond Port Augusta in South Australia. Sam had the day off and thought he'd indulge in a little horse riding. He approached one of the cockies (an all embracing term for the Australian bush worker) and asked where the horses were kept.

This was before Sam leapt to world fame in the lead role of the television series *Riley Ace of Spies* and movies such as *Dead Calm, A Cry In*

The Dark and *The Hunt For Red October*, but he was already well known on Australian screens. The cockie eyed him up and down. Sam Neill or not Sam Neill, he was as good as him any day.

'Over the hill,' he grunted.

Sam eyed him suspiciously.

'Any problems taking one for a bit of a ride?'

'Not if you can saddle it.'

'Yeah,' said Sam, and headed off, irritated at being treated like some city new chum. When he was almost out of earshot, he caught the cockie's parting words:

'And you've got enough time.'

He didn't know quite what to make of that, but he was damned

Sam Neill starred as John Ingram in the 1989 Warner Brothers' thriller *Dead Calm*

if he was going back to ask what it meant. He trudged into the silent heat, and eventually came to some horses in the shade of a horse float.

He says now that if he hadn't been so determined not to be taken for a mug by the cockie, he'd have had a good look around for the usual guard dog. As it was, he missed him; a mangy, ugly blue heeler, the world's best (and meanest) cattle dog. He had one eye, a couple of broken teeth, a half torn off ear and looked about as old as Methuselah. He was tied to a typical outback dog leash; a section of one inch chain, then a great heavy bit you could tow a truck with, then the inevitable length of wire attached to a frayed piece of rope that wouldn't hold a chihuahua. Only a madman would step inside the radius of that leash. A madman, or a careless actor.

Sam found a saddle, slammed the door and headed for the horses. They sighted each other at the same moment. Sam might have been careless, but he was no madman. The saddle hit the dirt as he hit the toe, the blue heeler on its feet and howling towards him, fangs bared, eyes aflame, the chain clanking at his tail. Sam made the length of the tether about two feet ahead of the dog. It was like a cartoon. The chain snapped tight – *clang, boy-ong*! The heeler's teeth were inches from his throat. Sam stared for one horror-stricken moment and took off again, the dog baying like the hound of the Baskervilles.

It had to happen. The weak link in the chain lasted just long enough for Sam to reach the top of the hill and to catch his breath. He hunched over, panting, just as the howls started getting closer again. Sam didn't look back. He raced to the only protection in sight – an old broken down truck at the side of the road. He dived into the front seat as the dog hit the side of the truck like a charging buffalo.

His relief at such a narrow escape was but momentary. He surveyed his predicament. Here he was trapped inside a baking metal coffin with the mercury around 130 degrees and a baying fiend outside waiting to kill him. Exhausted, helpless and terrified, Sam knew he'd disappear into a small puddle of perspiration before anyone found him. 'Here within lies poor Sam Neill, done to death by a mad blue heel.' He tried to raise a laugh, but it just wouldn't come. Neither did help. The dog settled back on its paws, staring at him. Time passed. They both dozed in the heat.

He was awakened by a thump at the window on the driver's side. Two bloodshot eyes in a grizzled, leather-brown, grey-bearded face peered at him.

'What are you doin' there? Waitin' for rain?'

Sam stared in disbelief and then horror, as the blue heeler woke baying for fresh blood.

'Holy suffering shit!' yelled Greybeard, yanking open the door and hurling himself into the driver's seat. 'Why didn't you tell me?'

'You didn't give me any time,' snapped Sam, suddenly in no mood for stupid questions. 'Now look what you've done. Woken the bloody thing up.'

'Strike a flamin' light,' said Greybeard, shaking his head. The dog dozed on its paws once more and they quietly pondered their plight. Then the old boy noticed something. The dog was off to one side and the last length of rope lay snaked across the track downhill from the truck's right-hand wheel. He nudged Sam.

'When I say go, let off the handbrake. Easy, mind.' Bewildered, Sam took the handbrake, wondering what the crazy old coot had planned.

There was no way that dog would stand for being run over. It would probably eat the truck.

'Now!' hissed Greybeard and Sam eased off the handbrake. The truck slowly rolled forward until the wheel was over the rope.

'Pull on the brake!' The truck jarred to a halt as the dog set up a frantic baying.

'You bloody little beauty,' chortled Greybeard, and without another word pushed open the door and headed over the ridge and out of sight. Sam figured the blue heeler would either strangle itself or break free at any moment.

Robert Grubb as the new slick city doctor, Dr Geoff Standish

'Now or never,' he yelled, leapt to the dirt and broke at least the four minute mile getting back to the film crew, where the cattle dogs were trained to behave politely and the cockies must never be asked any questions, ever, about anything.

'Anyhow,' said Robert, as he rounded off the yarn, 'I used to get a good laugh out of this and they stitched it into one of the scripts with Peter O'Brien as a young bushie, Sam Patterson, and I was the city slicker doctor who didn't know anything about cattle dogs. It really worked.'

It's all part of the true-to-life quality that puts *The Flying Doctors* in a different league from the standard soapie. His relationship with Lenore Smith's Sister Kate Wellings was typical. Like Robert's role, it grew largely from the actors' own input.

They both made it clear from the start they didn't want any romantic involvement, just two people who happened to be working together. They wanted to avoid the old doctor-nurse romantic cliché that inevitably degenerated into a screen marriage as soon as the ratings started to flag.

They felt, like everyone else on the series, that *The Flying Doctors* really had something going for it and they didn't want to diminish its potential. The scriptwriters went along with the idea and everything was hunkydory – at first.

Then they found an interesting development. To keep them emotionally apart the scripts started featuring lots of arguments between the two; snappy, bickering little things that in real life often disguise an attraction between two people.

Robert and Lenore suggested that they have a reconciliation where they realise they're actually quite alike and that's the reason they've been so stand-offish with each other. The director went along with the idea and they had three episodes where the two of them were constantly at each other's throats. Then they sat down and had a talk about it all and discovered how they really felt about each other and the romance, stormy as it was, eventually led to a classic screen wedding. It was one of those rare occasions where the actors virtually take over the direction of the plot from the writers and producers.

At one stage the acting was so torrid that rumours began that they were also a number off-screen, which, seeing as Robert was happily married, set the cat among the pigeons. He laughs about it now, but it brought home a few lessons.

'The business of on-screen romance is thrown at kids all the time and they think because it's happening there it has to continue off screen. It's all part of the nonsense that's fed to them every day. I have two kids, Emerson, aged eight and Hayden, aged five. I'm very careful about what they see on the television. I can't stand all this murder and mayhem. Even news bulletins seem preoccupied with violence and sudden death. The one programme I let them watch on television after 7.30 p.m. is *The Flying Doctors*, not because I'm in it, that tends to confuse them even more, but because it's wholesome viewing. But even that's not sacrosanct when you get the media hinting at romance that could break up the family. On-screen romance is nothing like that. Fair enough if you're single and you meet someone you're attracted to, but usually you end up just good friends. Or the opposite applies and there's something between the two of you that doesn't click, in which case romance is the last thing on your mind.

'You work as mates. You spend every day developing things together and it is a highly professional relationship; one that doesn't allow any escape or interruptions like romance. It is a funny sort of thing. You

Sister Kate Wellings (Lenore Smith) and Dr Geoff Standish (Robert Grubb), the doctor and nurse duo of the series

are invading someone else's space, touching, cuddling and kissing and you do become very close. I suppose because you are an actor the deeper implications don't apply just as a doctor can't afford to let himself get too emotionally involved with his patient.'

Whenever he feels himself perhaps losing control somewhere he always thinks of the story about Marlon Brando and Jack Nicholson after they'd had a terrific blow-up.

They were due to shoot a scene with a close-up of Brando talking to Nicholson. But Brando said it would be better not to have Nicholson actually in front of him at the time. Instead he selected a block of wood and spoke to that. He didn't want his antagonistic feelings captured by the cameras. Brando believed that no matter how good you were at masking your inner feelings, these things did leak onto the film somehow.

'Mind you, Brando could also have been having a go at Nicholson,' laughed Robert. 'Telling him he'd rather talk to a block of wood!'

A stormy romance led to a classic on-screen wedding for Dr Geoff Standish and Sister Kate Wellings

He's very strong on screencraft, which is another reason Robert likes *The Flying Doctors*. Because it's being shot on film, he only has one camera to deal with. He can't stand the multi-camera situation with people just sitting there and waiting for the lens to train on them.

'With these great hefty units swishing around all over the place you don't really know where the right one is at any time. There's a certain knack to knowing which camera the director is planning to use. You can find yourself acting your piece to the wrong camera and act yourself right out of the scene. You can also get the sense that someone's acting for one camera and you're acting for another. With a single camera it's set. You rehearse a couple of times and you do it and you know exactly what's going to pop up on the screen. As a person who has done a lot of stage work I believe you can channel all your energies into one area, in this case the camera.'

Happily, the role has also led to the possibility of Robert fulfilling his lifetime ambition – to act in Europe. *The Flying Doctors* is the top-rated

(opposite) Royal Flying Doctor aircraft returning to base

(opposite) Andrew
McFarlane as Dr Tom
Callaghan, the first Flying
Doctor in the series

(left) Lenore Smith and
Robert Grubb. Once
rumoured to be a pair off-
screen, as well as on

(opposite) Robert Grubb as Dr Geoff Standish in front of
the Coopers Crossing air base

(above) Mr and Mrs Sam Patterson, the pilot's and
the mechanic's wedding day

(opposite) Posing for the cameras – off-screen – Peter O'Brien and Rebecca Gibney

(left) Sam and Emma – the early days of their romance

(opposite) Reluctant heart-throb, Alex Papps, as Nick Cardaci a jack of all trades in the series

(left) Liz Burch as Dr Chris Randall

(opposite) Relaxing off-screen – Robert Grubb and Liz Burch

(left) Car mechanic Emma Plimpton, played by Rebecca Gibney, runs the Coopers Crossing garage

Vic and Nancy Buckley,
the Coopers Crossing
publicans – a perfect
match off-screen too

Brett Climo as Dr David
Ratcliffe, a young Flying
Doctor learning the ropes

(opposite) Pat Evison as
Violet Carnegie, the local
village gossip

Mark Neal as the young
Marty Jarvis

show in Holland and Belgium and popularity is climbing steadily in the United Kingdom and other European countries. He was flown to Holland last year to take part in a television spectacular and the Dutch were even planning to shoot a couple of episodes of one of their top sitcoms in Australia and have a visit from the Flying Doctor written into the script.

In Europe these days, he's seen as the typical Australian – which he is – playing out the adventures of a remarkable profession – which the Flying Doctor is. He's perfect for the part; craggy good looks, keen, penetrating eyes and a whimsical sense of humour. And he loves the outback and its people.

'It is a fascinating place full of very resourceful characters. I once read a book, *One Thousand Things to do with a Piece of Wire*. I loved that. Australians have a reputation as the world's greatest improvisers and that's where you see them at their best; inventing a myriad of different ways to endure in the harsh bush. Not that you have to be a bushie to be a great improviser.

'My father's got this nice little vegetable garden out the back of the house and whenever he goes to the rubbish dump he brings back more than he took down there. He came back one day with a whole lot of computer parts. Mum said, "What on earth are you going to do with those?" They were flat and small and silver and he strung them up over his lettuce and they'd flap around in the wind and keep all the birds away. I love that adaptability and of course you see it all the time out in the bush. You just have to go along and see their fences and their gates.

'The cockpit of the aircraft we fly in is on hydraulics in the studio and we used to have this little guy come around and pull levers and things and rock us all over the "sky". It was always breaking down and costing a fortune to get fixed up, so finally they got sick of it and they put it on tractor tyres with a piece of four by two underneath. A couple of stage hands would get on either end of this great big lever and wobble, wobble and off we'd go, up into the blue yonder. It worked out fine. We'd get in the cockpit and yell, "Yeah, that's great. More wobble please."'

It's got nothing to do with flying doctors, but don't be surprised if you see shiny beer bottle tops or even old engine parts strung across a Coopers Creek vegetable garden in some future episode.

(opposite) Demetris Goannidis (George Kapiniaris) or to those who know him, DJ, the radio operator at the Royal Flying Doctor's base

THE HEART-THROBS

Peter O'Brien took one look at Minyip and laughed. He wasn't mocking the town. He was not about to make Hicksville jokes which other actors, usually from Sydney, included in their repertoires. He was enjoying Minyip because it was not the small straggle of houses and buildings, complete with numbskull yokels, as had been described to him on more than one occasion. Compared to where he came from it was almost a metropolis. 'To me Minyip is a big town,' he observed. 'Where I grew up, in Jervois on the Murray River in South Australia, there was a water tank, a bowling green, a town hall, a footy oval and a tiny school. That was it. Minyip is much bigger than it looks on screen. I mean, the main street is bitumen!'

Now a star of the small screen, in fact an idol to many teenagers who surround him shrieking and screaming as though he's just had three hit records in a row, Peter sometimes goes back home for a weekend with his old mates. He described one occasion thus: 'On Saturday arvo [afternoon] I toss the coin at the footy, then on Saturday night there's a cabaret at the local hall. Great fun, bring-your-own plate, one of those evenings where, before you know it, you can't walk because all the beer's on the floor. None of the boys talk to the girls and at the end of the evening there's the obligatory two or three fights.'

Such is life in a small Australian country town. The clichés sit comfortably. The overseas image of unsophisticated Australia is reinforced. The city intellectuals hate it but they seldom journey from their natural habitats of gossipy bistros to see it and even if they did they wouldn't understand anything happening around them. You make your own fun in a small Australian country town and if that includes drinking too much and getting into fights forgotten next day, so be it.

Peter left Jervois, but not for ever, when he went to Melbourne in

1984 and got small parts in such television series as *Prisoners* and *Carson's Law*. On his own admission, he played hard and often lived rough, at one stage sharing a house with eleven others, which meant that a decent night's sleep was not high on his agenda. Then came the role of Shane Ramsay in *Neighbours*. In no time at all he was one of the most popular figures on Australian television, unable to walk up the street without, in his words, 'getting the shirt ripped off his back.'

Weary, and not a little wary, of the attention, he went to Britain and Europe in 1987. He thought he would have no difficulty walking down the street with his shirt intact, but had not realised that *Neighbours*, now screened by the BBC, was fast becoming the hottest show on television, as well as the most maligned. He found this out while wander-ing along Oxford Street, London, peering idly into shop windows and wondering if his budget would stretch to another shirt or two. 'Then I noticed a whole lot of people following me. I ducked into a shop. The owner hid me in a changing room and told the crowd I'd gone out the back way.'

Heart-throb and star of the small screen, Peter O'Brien

Neighbours hadn't yet reached Europe so he had no problems when he went across the channel. He slept on beaches, at airports, in cars. He hitch-hiked. He got into trouble.

On one occasion, in Greece, he was in a nightclub with two girls having a beer, generally enjoying himself and bothering no one. Trouble started when a local took a fancy to one of the girls.

'Come on, you dance,' he demanded in broken English.

'No, go way,' she said.

'Come on, come on,' he insisted.

'Push off,' she said flatly.

Ever the gentleman, because above all country lads have good manners, Peter told the man something similar. A knife appeared in the man's hand. Peter blinked, considered the seriousness of the situation and tried the charm that worked so well at home half a world away. It meant nothing to the Greek who was jabbing the air with the knife. He had never heard of *Neighbours*. Furthermore he was being addressed in a language so alien it could have been coming from someone from outer space. As Peter said later: 'I was really scared and it looked bad. All my wit and charm had run out and he was still threatening me. Finally the police arrived and chucked him in the slammer.'

On his return to Australia, he was offered the role of Sam Patterson in *The Flying Doctors* which the producers describe this way: 'A local boy, Sam Patterson learns to fly on the station his father manages. His quiet country ways, his friendliness and his ability as a pilot make him a favourite with the doctors and the townspeople . . . Sam has to prove

Peter as the Flying
Doctor's pilot, Sam
Patterson

himself over and over to gain a permanent position as the Royal Flying Doctor Service pilot, the only job he ever wanted to do. He establishes himself, not only as a good pilot, but a caring person who can assist the doctors in an emergency . . .'

Peter describes Sam in more down-to-earth terms. 'I like him as a character, but he's a bit of a dag. He's not a sophisticated city boy, he's a worker.' A little like Peter really.

When he first went on *The Flying Doctors* set he had butterflies in his stomach. There were two reasons. First of all he felt a trifle awed by the reputation of the series, which most actors and critics considered was a cut above the rest. 'My first day on the set I was so nervous I could hardly remember what the character was like. I was scared about what people were going to think of me and how they would react.' The second reason was that he hated flying, no small problem for an actor who has to clamber in and out of light aircraft the way other people get into their cars, and look confident while doing so. 'I'm the world's worst flyer. I always expect the worse when I get in a plane and I'm always grateful to touch down.'

Peter took the role in *The Flying Doctors* simply because he could not work forever in the sausage factory atmosphere of *Neighbours* churning out five half hours a week, even though it was a nice secure job. The Grundy Organisation, producers of *Neighbours*, tempted him with a fatter contract but he declined. He had to get his head onto a new show, had to develop his talents further than the cardboard character of Shane Ramsay. 'I could have easily sat in *Neighbours* and been content, but I needed a change. I don't think the character could have gone on any further and maintained credibility.'

There was another reason for the producers of *The Flying Doctors* wanting his name on a contract. The producers don't talk about the reason in public, but behind closed doors, during their planning conferences, they all agree that a heart-throb is what the show needs.

A heart-throb is a male with the kind of looks and physique which will draw female fans to the screen no matter what role he plays. If he can act, so much the better. Sometimes they are called sex symbols and have been around since the days of silent movies; Rudolph Valentino was a heart-throb, Tom Cruise is one today. Nothing changes except the hair-cuts.

'A heart-throb is a male with the kind of looks and physique which will draw female fans to the screen no matter what role he plays' – such is Peter O'Brien

Actors hate being called heart-throbs. They may quietly thank the great make-up artist in the sky that they were not born looking like the Hunchback of Notre Dame but they publicly detest the title. 'Heart-throbs come in and out of fashion like pointy shoes,' said Peter O'Brien. 'It's the media that makes you into one. If you can act then you don't have to worry. You should just concern yourself with the quality of your work and make sure each role is different.'

On sex symbols he has said much the same. 'It's so ridiculous. Jack Nicholson is the sort of sex symbol I could handle being, that is, fifty, fat, balding and still getting the great parts.'

His mother, Betty O'Brien, also doesn't see anything in her son that would be inclined to make the heart flutter. 'It doesn't really mean much to me,' she said when the subject was raised. 'He is just the same to me and no different to anyone else.'

But try telling that to the fans. Even though *The Flying Doctors* does not have the same high ratings as *Neighbours* the former, aiming for a

Off-screen romance; long-time girlfriend Elaine Smith (formerly of *Neighbours* fame) and Peter

family audience, Peter is still pursued by young females, anxious to obtain what their mothers have warned them about. 'People say I could have my pick,' he told the Australian fan magazine, *TV Week*. 'Sometimes I go out with mates and they tell me there are girls around, but I'm oblivious to all that. If a girl came up, stripped naked and propositioned me, I might be aware of it, but I don't go looking. It's my mates who do well out of the girls who come up and say hello to me. I edge away, but my mates carry on talking to them. I suppose I could exploit the position if I wanted to, but if I did I would get a reputation that would spread like wildfire. I've never been promiscuous. I'd rather have a few beers with my mates.'

Nor does the media, the British media in particular, take notice of his protestations. With both *Neighbours* and *The Flying Doctors* screening in Britain, he has been pursued by the London press as if he was the biggest exclusive story of the year. In no time at all they had him all but married to his long-time girlfriend, Elaine Smith, a regular on *Neighbours*. She was astonished at the attention she received during a visit to London. 'There were only two things they really wanted to know,' she said. 'One was about my relationship with Peter. The other was how much money it would take for me to strip.'

Caring little for the laws relating to bigamy, the press had him all but married to two women at once. One newspaper claimed he was about to wed Rebecca Gibney, his co-star on *The Flying Doctors*. 'This was quite remarkable because she was getting engaged to someone else at the time,' he said.

Peter kept finding media representatives in the most astonishing places. Had one popped up from beneath his bed he wouldn't have been surprised. They followed him in cars, loitered like suspicious persons around his hotel and hid themselves in corridors. 'It's outrageous,' he said. 'When you arrive, it's like you're from Mars. Any bit of dirt they can find, they'll go digging for it.' The Australian press, on the other hand, treats the soapie stars in a more casual fashion.

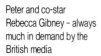

Peter and co-star Rebecca Gibney – always much in demand by the British media

Australian reporters often have the telephone numbers of the stars and ring them every now and again for a chat or run into them at social functions.

The British fans weren't far behind the media. Peter was mobbed by fans at Heathrow Airport and the car of BBC publicist, Carol Millward, was in danger of being demolished when he was driven to the Terry Wogan Show. Millward recalled: 'He has hundreds of female admirers here and about a hundred people climbed over my car to get to him after the Wogan appearance. I think he was a bit surprised at how popular the show is but you know Peter, he's so laid back he's not affected by the star treatment.'

Rebecca Gibney, less used to such attention, was amazed. 'It was pretty scary when all those girls tried to get at him. I got my hair pulled in the scramble and our driver got punched in the face. Pete's pretty modest and doesn't take the sex symbol tag to heart.'

When he returned in 1989, to play in a pantomime, *Mother Goose*,

Peter on the Terry Wogan Show in 1988. Afterwards he was mobbed by adoring female fans outside television theatre

and a stage production of *Butterflies are Free*, he found the media were no less anxious to get his name in print, even if the stories had little foundation in the truth, or even none at all. One newspaper reported he got into a rage and chased three teenagers who had arrived at his house seeking autographs. Then he drove after them in his car. It made a nice little story, but Peter gave his version. 'We hired a farm house. Once word got out that we were living there, the kids really did give me a hard time, even peering through windows. One day I came out and explained that we signed autographs at the theatre and to please not come into our yard. A couple of days later it was in the paper that I had threatened people and even tried to run a mother and family down in my high-powered Datsun. Just because I have a beaten-up VW and didn't threaten anyone makes no difference (to the British press).'

Even Peter's parents were not able to escape the British media's hell bent pursuit of something other than truth. Jack and Betty O'Brien were at home one day when there was a knock at the door.

Introducing himself, a British journalist inquired if the O'Briens would like to talk about their son. 'Sorry, mate,' said Jack, who although affable was wary of talking to anyone from the media. 'You better see Peter's agent.'

The O'Briens thought they would hear no more. But they hadn't taken into account the reporter's ingenuity, not to mention his imagination. Soon afterwards a story appeared in a British newspaper claiming Jack was battling cancer. 'Peter doesn't know whether dad Jack will live or die,' said the story. 'The whole family is on tenter-hooks waiting for the doctor's life or death verdict.'

Jack O'Brien was sickened. Five years earlier he'd had cancer of the bowel, but two operations had cleared him of the disease. 'I've never felt better in my life,' was his reaction to the story. 'Right now I'm as fit as a fiddle.'

But there were more 'exclusives' in the story. It went on to claim that Peter was 'terrified' that if he had any children they, too, might be 'cot-death victims like his elder brother.'

Betty O'Brien was upset and dismayed. She told the Australian publication, *Woman's Day*: 'We realised we would have to expect stories in the press about Peter when he became well known. But this story is the worst yet. I speak from my heart when I say I'm utterly sickened and horrified. Like many women, I had a stillborn baby. That's the true story. It's not an experience anyone wants to talk about, is it?'

Therein lies the danger of being a heart-throb. A heart-throb cannot be a person of ordinary failings, of commonplace background, of average ambitions and yearnings. His life must be lived according to the 'Dictionary of Superlatives'. His ways must be unlike those of lesser mortals. Everything about him must read like a script from a soap opera.

Peter O'Brien understands the heart-throb business. He might not like it but realises he is in an industry where idols must have their day, even if some do not contain twenty-four hours. Alex Papps, on the other hand, admits to being bewildered by media attention, and at a loss to know why it should be focused on him.

Rumours of an off-screen liaison between Peter and Rebecca were splashed all over English newspapers and magazines

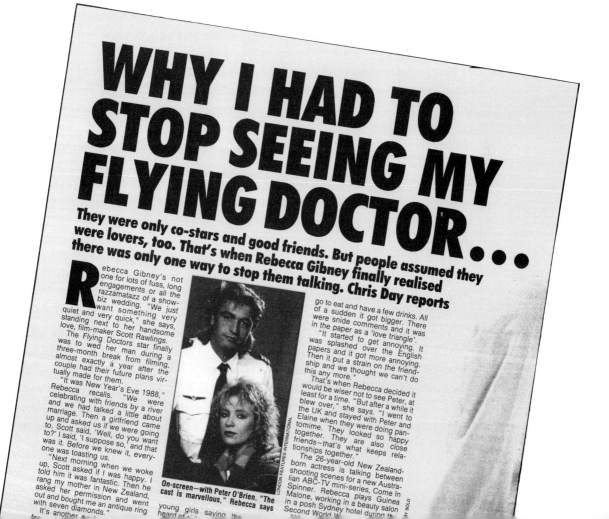

WHY I HAD TO STOP SEEING MY FLYING DOCTOR...

They were only co-stars and good friends. But people assumed they were lovers, too. That's when Rebecca Gibney finally realised there was only one way to stop them talking. Chris Day reports

Rebecca Gibney's not one for lots of fuss, long engagements or all the razzamatazz of a show-biz wedding. "We just want something very quiet and very quick," she says, standing next to her handsome love, film-maker Scott Rawlings.

The Flying Doctors star finally was to wed her man during a three-month break from filming, almost exactly a year after the couple had their future plans virtually made for them.

"It was New Year's Eve 1988," Rebecca recalls. "We were celebrating with friends by a river and we had talked a little about marriage. Then a girlfriend came up and asked us if we were going to. Scott said, 'Well, do you want to?' I said, 'I suppose so,' and that was it. Before we knew it, everyone was toasting us.

"Next morning when we woke up, Scott asked if I was happy. I told him it was fantastic. Then he rang my mother in New Zealand, asked her permission and went out and bought me an antique ring with seven diamonds."

It's another

go to eat and have a few drinks. All of a sudden it got bigger. There were snide comments and it was in the paper as a 'love triangle'.

"It started to get annoying. It was splashed over the English papers and it got more annoying. Then it put a strain on the friendship and we thought we can't do this any more."

That's when Rebecca decided it would be wiser not to see Peter, at least for a time. "But after a while it blew over," she says. "I went to the UK and stayed with Peter and Elaine when they were doing pantomime. They looked so happy together. They are also close friends—that's what keeps relationships together."

The 26-year-old New Zealand-born actress is talking between shooting scenes for a new Australian ABC-TV mini-series, Come In Spinner. Rebecca plays Guinea Malone, working in a beauty salon in a posh Sydney hotel during the Second World W...

On-screen—with Peter O'Brien. "The cast is marvellous," Rebecca says

young girls saying the heard of ...

LONDON FEATURES INTERNATIONAL

And it is. When he attended a country race meeting he was astonished to find trailing behind him a gaggle, or perhaps a goggle, of small boys, starry-eyed girls of all ages and not a few of their mothers, their Instamatics at the ready, and all wanting autographs. 'It's a very strange feeling,' he said. 'It's nice to know that people react to what you do, but I don't really know how to cope with it. I remember when it started to happen. I found it was strange to think people knew about you and saw your face in magazines.'

Being a sensible young man, Alex sat down and let the subject loose in his mind for a while. He knew he was placed on a pedestal because of his role in the soapie, *Home and Away*. He appreciated that if he was selling socks in a department store no one would be demanding his autograph. 'The way I've worked it out is that the person who is being seen in the magazines or on television is a totally separate part of me. That is the way I'm trying to stay detached from it. I think I have to try and maintain the separation from what is the television person and what is me.'

He often tried to explain who he really was, that away from the television screen he was not the character, Frank Morgan, but a young bloke called Alex Papps who happened to have taken up acting as a career. 'I'm the person who dags around at home, watches television and orders home delivery pizza, yet I'm portrayed as something completely different.'

He tried to explain but no one was listening. He couldn't move without being swamped by fans; they even crawled through the windows of his small apartment. Sometimes, out of sheer frustration, he would deny his identity when approached for an autograph, a ruse that fooled no one, especially the fans. And always the tag he detested, the label of heart-throb, would be attached to his name. He would pick up a magazine and read a story about himself, which invariably began: 'Heart-throb Alex Papps. . .'

He would wince once again. 'I hate the whole idea of being a heart-throb. What's a heart-throb? I am an actor. I can't cope with the idea of people who don't know me saying they love me or they hate me because I'm in the public eye. It's nice to have fans and have recognition. That is always a good thing. But it is easier to accept people liking you because of your acting than because they think you are a spunk.'

After a while Alex could take it no longer. The pressure of always being in the public eye, of being unable to move without being hounded, became too much. He was sick of going on promotional trips to shopping centres, being jostled, hassled, mauled, even grabbed by precocious young females on parts of the body generally considered private. Even though he enjoyed doing the soap, liked the cast and welcomed the security, he felt he had to get out of *Home and Away*.

Before *Home and Away* he had worked in *The Henderson Kids*, a family situation series, and had a small part in *Neighbours* before it became internationally famous and began worrying the British critics. After twelve months in *Home and Away* he received an offer he felt was too good to refuse. A week later he turned up on the set of *The Flying Doctors*.

Alex Papps as Frank Morgan in *Home and Away*

He felt enormous relief.

'I want to develop as an actor, not a celebrity . . . There is nothing more dangerous than believing your own publicity . . . Sure, it's flattering to have people write to you and compliment you. But I don't judge my worth by the number of magazine covers I appear on. I go on how I feel when I am working and whether I'm learning anything or advancing. . . It was very risky leaving a high-profile programme like *Home and Away*. But you have to take risks. I knew I was leaving security for a big question mark, but that's the nature of the acting business and I wanted to move on and do other things.'

Another point he saw in his favour was that *The Flying Doctors* was a mere one hour a week; *Home and Away* filled two and a half hours a week. His heaviest day on *The Flying Doctors* could involve five scenes; in *Home and Away* he could do twenty scenes in one day. Now he had time to develop his character, Nick Cardaci, a jack-of-all-trades, who does a bit of driving, gardening and crop-spraying, helps Emma (Rebecca Gibney) at the garage and wants to make money to support his ailing father, mother and sisters. 'He is a likeable bloke, who is sensible and practical,' said Alex. 'Nick is more intelligent and together than Frank Morgan in *Home and Away*.'

But even when moving from one studio to another, from Sydney where *Home and Away* was made to Melbourne, Alex could not totally escape the heart-throb business. On his first day on the set of *The Flying Doctors* he was confronted by another victim in the form of Terence Donovan, father of the incredibly popular Jason. In an ironic twist, Terence was playing Jim Cardaci, Nick's father, a long-distance truck driver who, because of the many miles he travels, takes too many amphetamines. The two actors had much to compare and were able to look at the heart-throb business from two completely different angles.

Terence Donovan has been an actor for more than thirty years, gainfully employed not only in many Australian television series but in films and on the stage. However, he was virtually unknown outside his country until Britain decided Jason was the best thing to come along in many seasons, or at least since the previous pop phenomenon. Terence was living in the leafy quietness of suburban Melbourne, watching his son develop from a cardboard cut-out in *Neighbours* into

Father and son, Terence and Jason Donovan. Terence plays Nick Cardaci's father in an episode of *The Flying Doctors*

a pop singer and more serious actor. He knew Jason was a big name but not how big until his peace was shattered by the incessant ringing of his telephone. It rang so much he had to change the telephone number he had had for twenty years, which none too pleased him. 'I was rather fond of that number,' he said. Most of the calls were from overseas correspondents desperate for a new angle on Jason, if indeed a new angle existed.

'The European paparazzi would ring me up at all hours of the day and night, friendly as anything, but very obviously after a story about Jason,' he told Jenni Gilbert, of the Sydney *Daily Telegraph*. 'It became a bit too much. I'd never really understood the popularity of *Neighbours* and the huge success my son has had over in Europe until I started getting all these calls. I knew Jason was going to fly high and do well because he has youth on his side, a good look about him and the ability and skill to be able to carry it through. None of us in the business even ten years ago were lucky enough to get that sort of exposure overseas. So maybe my peers and I paved the way for Jason and Kylie [Minogue] and their success.'

Alex Papps was nervous when he went on to the set of *The Flying Doctors*, as are many who have made the transition from soapie to series. Some consider *The Flying Doctors* to be little more than a soapie, but there are differences, although not enough to provide material for an all-night argument. Soapies use a camera technique that requires close-ups and extreme close-ups. The viewer is a witness to the stylised emotions; expressions of pity, jealousy, rage and self-doubt. Time is prolonged yet little happens, no character becomes so important they cannot be written out, there is an economy of narrative and conventional objects such as a telephone or a door bell take on major significance. Also each episode in a soapie should end with one or more characters, if not hanging over a cliff, at least getting close to the edge. There should be more loose ends than on a plate of spaghetti. A series usually tells a complete story in one episode, sometimes two, but never longer.

Actors in series tend to look down a trifle on their soapie colleagues, but they shouldn't because most began their careers in the lather of five half hours a week. Alan Batemen, former head of drama for the Nine Network, which screens *The Flying Doctors* in Australia, will have none of this snobbery. 'I don't see "soap" as a derogatory term,' he said. '*Brideshead Revisited* was a soap opera. So was *The Forsyte Saga*. So were *The Pallisers* and *Upstairs, Downstairs*. There are wonderfully cute terms like "contemporary serial" and "Australian drama series" but it's really a way of categorising.'

Whatever he was appearing in, whether it be soapie or series, Alex Papps turned up on a Monday morning to work on an established show, playing a new character, with an unfamiliar cast. He knew some of the faces, such as Rebecca Gibney, Robert Grubb and Lenore Smith, having met them at functions. In Australia's relatively small show business circle one would have to live as a hermit not to meet actors from various series at functions. Still, he was nervous. 'Then the first person I spotted was a technician who turned out to be an old friend from my days on *The Henderson Kids*. Another person I knew from *The Henderson Kids* doubled as my stuntman for a horse race scene. It was a great relief to see familiar faces.'

Aware of the difficulty in entering an established series, of being the new boy on the block, the other actors gave Alex a welcome party that travelled around the clubs of Melbourne until the milkman hours of the morning. Alex's doubts disappeared. He knew he had made the right decision and at last felt comfortable in his chosen profession. His writing hand, that had signed so many autographs felt better already. 'It's nice to have the focus taken off you,' he said. 'It's good to be able to sit back and know everybody is not looking at me because it is an ensemble cast. I am not the centre of attention. I haven't been brought on this show to smile for the cameras every ten seconds and hope people are swooning.'

In contrast, Brett Climo, who plays Dr David Ratcliffe in *The Flying Doctors*, is not sure whether he is a heart-throb or not. The fans have no doubts. One girl who got his home telephone number thought two o'clock in the morning a fine time to make calls. 'Then she started

Heart-throb or not? Brett Climo as Dr David Ratcliffe, the young Flying Doctor learning the ropes

sending letters saying I was leading her on simply by answering the phone,' said Brett, still amazed he could attract such intense infatuation.

He is equally amazed people should bother to write letters to him. Fan letters. Letters full of gushing adoration. Letters from strangers. 'It's hard to talk about without sounding patronising, and I really respect what they're saying. It's great to know that your work has actually had an effect on people, that it inspired them to sit down and write something. I answer all the letters. I didn't think I would, but I do. You just can't ignore people when they go to that much trouble for you.'

Neither, incidentally, does Peter O'Brien ignore the mail that he

receives, which boosts Australia Post's revenue by as many as 500 letters a week. His mother, Betty, helps with the letters, although she has learned that the content of some envelopes can be steamy. Fans tend to put thoughts down on paper they would never express verbally. 'I don't like reading the letters because some are quite personal,' said Betty, diplomatically.

Maybe the reason for Brett Climo's surprise at all that is happening around and to him comes from the fact he was never consumed by the desire to be an actor, at least not in his younger days. He never entertained his family by wearing a lampshade on his head and using a soup ladle for a microphone. He wasn't sure what he wanted to be as he grew up in Sydney's southern suburbs. Not until he was seventeen. He looked around, saw there was a job called acting and decided to 'have a shot at it'. Taking a day off school, he found an agent and was given a small part in a film, *The Times They Are A Changing*.

He found it not a bad job at all. But to this day he does not see acting as the world's greatest occupation, perhaps agreeing with Spencer Tracy who put it this way: 'Why do actors think they're so goddam important? They're not. Acting is not an important job in the scheme of things. Plumbing is.'

Brett Climo put it his way in a conversation with Sydney show business writer, Kevin Sadlier: 'Acting is not the best time I have in my life. Never has been. I mean, I enjoy it immensely and I'm glad I get paid to do it. And as long as I get paid to do it and as long as I get better at it, then I'm pleased about that. But the best times for me happen when I'm not working.'

Without formal training in dramatic acting, Brett followed a variation of the instructions originally given by the great American thespian, Alfred Lunt: 'Don't bump into the furniture and remember your lines.'

Said Brett: 'I could always remember my lines but I always bumped into the furniture. It was so difficult to do both things at the same time.'

Nevertheless he succeeded. He landed a role in *Sons and Daughters*, one of Australia's more primitive soapies, then had parts in *Archer*, a telemovie about Australia's greatest passion, The Melbourne Cup horse race, and the mini-series, *Vietnam*, in which he was blown up by a land mine. But at times he had doubts about acting, becoming despondent as he wondered if there was more to life than pretending to be someone else. 'You start questioning the reason why you want to work, and it was good for me to do that.'

Then came *A Country Practice*, a series or soapie (call it what you wish) that carries the same sort of prestige as *The Flying Doctors*. He played a nurse. He enjoyed the experience, the satisfaction of good ratings and the critics' applause but pined for something else. He wasn't sure exactly what he wanted, as long as it was a character different from the do-gooder image of *A Country Practice*. 'I'd like a complete change and be a hippie, a druggie or a murderer.'

He wasn't to be any of these. Instead, he graduated from nurse to doctor in *The Flying Doctors*, an achievement accomplished in a few weeks, making it possibly the quickest leap forward in the history of medicine. His character, Dr David Ratcliffe, is the son of a wealthy grazier who has returned to the country after studying medicine. Brett welcomed the change. 'I'm fairly lazy by nature and things can become a bit routine to me. I suppose I did get a little stale and saw this as a great chance to move on.'

The Flying Doctors also gave him freedom to develop the character. Because each episode is self-contained, he treated them as short telemovies produced once a week. Another reason he fitted comfortably into *The Flying Doctors* was that it was shot on film, a technique most experienced actors prefer. Working with video may mean there is a safety-net, the scene can be replayed instantly and if there are mistakes they can be shot again with little further expense. But it removes much of the challenge that actors working in film face daily. 'With film we don't know how it's actually going to look until it's cut together and put on the screen,' he said. 'So you've got this feeling of nervousness, and everyone's sort of focused on the same action, with a real sense of being in it together, and I like that.'

There was one other reason why he was pleased when offered a role in *The Flying Doctors*, a reason most actors understand. 'It's nice for the ego when that sort of thing happens,' he admitted.

The heart-throbs have their place in *The Flying Doctors*. But the series is an equal-opportunity employer. It is not male dominated. Females are not mere decorations but are also given meaty roles. They also have to share the same discomforts.

LIZ AND REBECCA

Hell, it was cold. Her teeth chattered as though they were driven by an electric motor, her hands shook, her nose felt it belonged to someone else. Liz Burch could not remember ever feeling so cold. Yet she was supposed to be in the outback with sweat pouring off her face, out there in the heart of Australia with the heat, dust and flies, where a person can die in two days if stranded without water. She was in no danger of dying from dehydration, of 'doing a perish' as they say in the outback. She was getting more water than she ever wanted to see again, gallons of the stuff pouring down on her from the freezing belly of a water tanker.

She swore under her breath. Then she laughed. When she had taken the role of Dr Chris Randall in *The Flying Doctors* she had thought, per-haps carelessly, that she would be working where the sun seldom stopped shining and where, if the temperature fell below seventy degrees, it was a cold day.

Instead, she was filming in Minyip in the middle of winter. It was 4 am and the clothes she and Lenore Smith (Sister Kate Wellings) were wearing were more suitable for the tropics. To add insult to injury, or bitterness to bleakness, they had to suck ice blocks to condense the moisture in their breath. It wouldn't look right for them to exhale small white puffs as though they were playing Eskimos.

'It's a glamorous life, ain't it?' someone said. No one laughed.

According to the scriptwriter, who wasn't feeling cold at all when putting the words on paper, Liz and Lenore had to carry a patient from the Flying Doctor aircraft to an ambulance during a rainstorm. To ensure the rain was not dropping gently from the heavens, or at least from a hose attached to the water tanker, a wind machine produced a miniature gale to add to their misery.

They did one take. 'I'm afraid we'll have to shoot it again,' said the

director. 'There was water on the lens.'

So they did it again. They picked up the stretcher carrying the patient, who Liz estimated weighed about nineteen stone – although the miserable conditions may have caused her to exaggerate his bulk – and went through the performance for a second time. As they staggered through the 'rain', their hands slipped from the stretcher handles made greasy by the water. Their burden thumped to the ground, yelling blue murder, and they raced for cover.

'We'll have to do that again, thank you.'

Eventually one of the prop men donned oilskins and gave them a hand, pretending he was a farmer who just happened to be wandering past in the middle of the night.

(above left) Liz Burch, Andrew McFarlane and Lenore Smith – the airborne medics

(above right) 'Since the age of four I've always dreamed of becoming an actress . . .' Liz Burch who plays Dr Chris Randall

At last they got the patient where they wanted him. Another scene which had to be shot involved sawing off one of the patient's legs with a hack-saw. Not his real leg, of course. *The Flying Doctors* strives for authenticity but cutting off a thespian's leg is frowned on by Actors' Equity, even on double rates. To add realism, a water pistol full of fake blood was squirted into Liz's face as she sawed away. The scene over, Liz, freezing cold, her face splattered with 'blood', laughed, walked outside and washed herself down in the 'rain'.

Unfortunately, their toil was in vain. The amputation scene never made it to the screen, the producers deciding it was not appropriate viewing for 7.30 p.m. in the evening.

After observing the misery of working in Minyip in winter, Pamela Bone, of the *Melbourne Age* newspaper, wrote: 'Watching the cast in the small town of Minyip was for me another shattering of the myth of stardom. The wind blowing off the Wimmera wheatfields down the main street of Minyip must have had a chill factor of about zero degrees . . . the discomfort level was approaching physical pain.'

It's not easy being a doctor in *The Flying Doctors*. They face problems unknown to the general practitioner. For one scene Liz was required to administer an injection to a girl patient. To give authenticity and yet save the actor's skin from becoming a pin cushion, a piece of wood was placed under the patient's shirt, allowing Liz to jab away with total confidence. But the needle jammed in the wood. Liz wrenched it with such force it leapt from her hand and somersaulted sharp-end first into the patient's leg.

She leaped to her feet, screaming: 'You bloody bitch, you're trying to kill me!'

Such is show business. Liz can barely remember a time when she didn't want to be in the business that would later have her tail frozen off at four in the morning. 'Since the age of four I've always dreamed of becoming an actress, a star, the best actress in the world . . . I found I could make people laugh. I could say dumb things, get words mixed up and people would laugh at me, and with me.'

A year later she wrote to the ABC, the Australian equivalent to the BBC, volunteering to work for the children's radio programme, *The Argonauts*; any job, from sweeping floors to cleaning toilets. They wrote back politely suggesting she wait until she was a little older.

'It's not easy being a doctor in *The Flying Doctors*. They face problems unknown to the general practitioner.' Liz in front of the Coopers Crossing air base

Undeterred, Liz studied drama at her Sydney school and at sixteen got her first role as Snow White in a pantomime. Things got tough after that. She had to play opposite a dog in *The Tinder Box* and any actor will tell you dogs not only never remember their lines but they steal the scenes. After appearing in a couple of revues at a Sydney hotel, she toured the club circuit with the eccentric entertainer, Tiny Tim. Her role was to dance in a little frilly dress while he went through a medley of eighty-six songs.

A bleak period followed, a time known in show business as actor's drought. She worked as a barmaid, an usherette, a book-keeper, wondering if perhaps acting was the right career for her. She was about to give it up and find a 'proper' job, when she found work with a game

show, *Winner Take All* – not the greatest role for an aspiring actor but one that kept the rent collector at bay. Then came a meaty, continuing part in the police drama series, *Cop Shop*. It was the biggest break in her career, a chance to establish her name, to fulfil her childhood ambitions. But she couldn't handle it, the pressures, the hype, the so-called glamour. 'I sort of buggered up my life a bit. I lost a lot of friends through being a bit of a loudmouth and being self-centred. I never worked hard enough and I was terrible in the series.'

After eighteen months she left *Cop Shop* and departed into a lonely life. Many people she thought were friends turned their backs on her, although the regular actors in *Cop Shop* stayed with her, helping when they could. For two years she could not find another acting job. Her confidence shattered, she worked in a furniture store, an experience she thought she would hate but which proved invaluable when she came into contact with ordinary, nine-to-five people. It taught her never to believe in her own publicity. A role as understudy for the stage comedy, *Noises Off*, allowed her to look again at her craft. Then came the lead in the adventure series, *Five Mile Creek*, co-produced by Walt Disney Studios.

Her work in *Five Mile Creek* attracted the attention of Crawford Productions who offered her the role of Dr Chris Randall, a single woman who had dedicated her life to the Royal Flying Doctor Service. The bad days were behind her. 'At this stage in my life I think I'm one of the luckiest people around,' she said soon after signing her contract.

She and Rebecca Gibney became close friends. They were known as the twins, sharing a larrikin* streak. 'When you work with people so closely for so long you develop almost a second language. You just know what the other person is going to say, particularly if you are acting together. Actors are very insecure human beings. It's great to have people around you can trust.'

Her life was settled. Her work was all she had hoped it would be, with the possible exception of certain winter days in Minyip. She was surrounded by people she knew were friends, and her bank manager was happy. 'A long run is good if you use it properly and you're still interested in what you're doing,' she told Karen Lateo of the Sydney *Sunday*

---

* larrikin: young person full of mischief.

Telegraph. 'I think there are two things to do if you're in a series: to save all the money you possibly can, which I've done – I've bought myself a flat and I own it – the other is to work as hard as you can at your craft. I've been very lucky because it's a role very different to me. She's very serious. I've been able to use that. I think I'm a hundred times better actor than I ever was.'

Perhaps her life was too good for whoever it is that decides our fate. Quite suddenly her blue bird of happiness fell from the sky. She wasn't to discover until later, of course, that in some ways her private life would be reflected in an episode of *The Flying Doctors*. The writers had Dr Randall surviving a horrifying plane crash and then having to contend with the grief of losing someone very close to her.

The episode was the last for the year, a fine piece of drama to bring viewers back the following season. Tired after a year's work, Liz was looking forward to the break. But her peace was shattered by the breakdown of a long love affair. Worse was to come. She learned that her forty-one-year-old sister, Rosemary, had contracted a rare skin disease – scleroderma – which caused the skin to tighten and become hard, resulting in a stiffening of the joints and leading to a gradual wasting of the muscles. She died soon afterwards. 'I didn't even know such a disease existed,' Liz said. 'There was nothing they could do for her.'

As Christmas drew near, Liz was close to breaking point. She didn't know which way to go or who to turn to. One day her telephone rang and on the line from London was her former *Flying Doctors* co-star, Andrew McFarlane, who had been in Britain for six months.

'Get on a plane and come over here,' he said. 'It'll do you the world of good.'

After considering it for a while, she couldn't think of a good reason for not going and caught the next available flight to London. The first thing she knew was that she had found a place colder than Minyip; London was going through its severest winter for fifty years. She and Andrew played like kids in the snow and within days she was not only feeling better but had also regained her inner strength. 'Andrew was a great comfort. He was absolutely magnificent. When Andrew and I get together – regardless of how long a break there's been – we just click in with each other. We really are great mates.'

Liz and Andrew have what could be called an interesting relationship. At times they thoroughly enjoy each other's company, at other
times they drive each other around the twist. Andrew put it this way:
'Liz is great fun to be with, we have very similar interests, live similar
lives. She is certainly, outside my family, the only person I can discuss
absolutely anything with. We never plan anything when we are
together, things just happen. We eat, talk, have a drink, talk more,
watch videos. It is never dull when Liz is around. I really think Liz is
like a jigsaw puzzle. There are times when I could smack her and
scream she is selfish and pig-headed. Then there are times when she is
the most loving and caring person I have ever met.'

Back in Australia and back in *The Flying Doctors*, Liz became
involved in a project that was to change her life. So emotional and
traumatising was it that she had to seek help from a psychiatrist and
considered giving up work on *The Flying Doctors*. On behalf of World
Vision she went to Ethiopia to make a documentary on its starving
children. When she returned she was haunted by what she had seen:
children with swollen bellies, legs like matchsticks, faces made gro-
tesque by hunger, empty eyes – figures from a nightmare.

'I was in such a state,' she told Bunty Avieson, of *Woman's Day*. 'No
one could get through to me. I had been through a huge trauma and I
was angry. Angry with my family, my friends and with World Vision for
abandoning me once we got back to Australia and leaving me to cope
on my own. There was no point in talking to my family and friends
because I just upset them. So I went along twice a week and cried for
an hour to a psychiatrist. I told him how angry I was with everybody,
how I didn't like working on *The Flying Doctors* any more, how I felt
fat. Eventually it came down to "Okay, so you feel guilty". We talked
over everything and it kind of freed me. The trip was so emotionally
draining it took me a year to come to terms with it.'

But come to terms with it she did, helped when 5 500 people each
promised to sponsor a child after the documentary was screened on
television. The guilt was still there (she feels it can never be completely
erased) but at least now she could face up to the harsh realities of third
world poverty. She agreed to go back to Africa, and to Bangladesh, for
World Vision. The memories of her second trip remain vivid but now
she is able to cope with the horrors she saw, the madness of a world

that has mountains of food in Europe and the United States, yet allows children elsewhere to die of starvation.

Some memories are bitter-sweet. In Bangladesh 200 children gathered around, silent, their big eyes staring. Liz wanted to communicate.

'This isn't getting anywhere,' she said to the film crew. 'Maybe a song will break through.'

There in the dust of a strange and tragic land, an unimaginable world away from the prosperity of her own country, she sang an old Australian children's song, *The Kookaburra Sits on the Old Gum Tree*. When she finished singing the children applauded and laughed. The

Liz in Africa on behalf of World Vision, a project which she claims has changed her life

international language of music was working, as it always does. The children shyly drew closer. Liz sang the first line of *Baa Baa Black Sheep*, then got the children to parrot the line. In no time at all they had learned the simple song and were singing it with gusto and, for a while, they forgot their empty bellies.

Sometimes she was reminded of how small the world really is, that the global village is upon us. Arriving in a small Ugandan village, miles from anywhere, which in European terms would be considered a civilised town, she heard a song coming from a tape-recorder. It

Brett Climo also became heavily involved with Liz's third world project

sounded familiar. No, it couldn't be! But it was – Kylie Minogue singing *The Locomotion*.

She journeyed on. In a Kenyan slum she met a deserted mother, Jacinta, and her daughter, Hannah. Jacinta owed A$75 on a piece of land in the country which would take her years to pay off.

'Jacinta wanted to move Hannah out of the slums so that she would have a better chance in life than she had had,' said Liz. 'We went into her tiny house and it was very neat, with flowers and a picture of Jesus on the wall. She gave me a hand-embroidered wall-hanging. I'd been fine until then. I thought, God, I have everything and she could sell this to make money. I walked outside and thought I'm not going to pretend any more and I just sobbed and sobbed. I looked up and there were about twenty children standing staring at me. They looked bewildered. They couldn't understand what they had done to upset me.' Liz and the film crew gave Jacinta her A$75, adding A$150 towards the cost of building her new home away from the slums.

Liz became almost completely preoccupied with promoting World Vision. She convinced co-star Brett Climo of its worth and also roped in Rebecca Gibney, who plays Emma Plimpton, the feisty garage mechanic in *The Flying Doctors*. Liz and Rebecca were known as the 'twins' by many working on the series, not only because they were far from the end of the queue where good looks were concerned but also because of their close friendship.

Rebecca got her role in *The Flying Doctors* because she wanted it badly. She thought about the audition for some time, deciding the best way would be to appear looking like a garage mechanic and not the stereotyped image of an actress carefully made-up and coiffured. Crawfords knew her work but she had to convince them she could play an earthy role. She wore dirty shorts and a baggy T-shirt, no make-up and her hair looked as though she had just got out of bed.

'You've got the part.' Crawfords told her.

A couple of years later, when going for an audition in the important ABC production, *Come in Spinner*, a mini-series set in Sydney during World War II, she used the same trick. Borrowing a dress from the old series, *The Sullivans*, also set in World War II, and with hair-style and make-up to match, she went off to audition.

'You've got the part.' the ABC told her.

Rebecca, twenty-six, grew up in Wellington, New Zealand, one of six children. It wasn't an easy life. Her father was an alcoholic, who was destroyed by a circulatory disease which led to the amputation of a limb and a long-drawn-out and painful death. Rebecca was sixteen. 'I had to look after him. I didn't really know him well until then. I got to know him as we sat each day watching daytime soap operas. That was about all he was able to do towards the end. When he died I went through some huge changes. I became very rebellious for quite a while.'

She went from job to job, unsure of her future, not caring too much about it anyway. She sold jewellery and did a little modelling before concluding that acting seemed a more interesting job than working behind a store counter. She landed several small jobs on New Zealand television. She was soon in demand and did what any ambitious New

Zealander does, fly across the Tasman Sea to Australia.

She was nineteen, with enough confidence to walk off the street into the office of a Melbourne theatrical agent who looked her up and down, noted her experience, albeit in the small pond of New Zealand television, and put her on the books. Two auditions came to nothing. Her confidence was sapped and she retired, slightly bruised, back to New Zealand. Two weeks before Christmas the telephone rang. It was the agent with offers of parts in two television series. She chose the Crawford children's series, *The Zoo Family*. A movie, *I Live With Me Dad*, followed.

Then came the role of Emma Plimpton in *The Flying Doctors* who saves Hurtle Morrison's garage from sinking beneath a load of debt. 'When Emma arrives, the garage is very sloppy and in a real financial state. Hurtle has drawers full of bills and he's been running it like a real

Rebecca Gibney who plays Emma Plimpton, the pretty yet tough garage mechanic

The long-awaited wedding day arrives for Emma Plimpton and Sam Patterson, the popular young couple of the series

country garage, three chooks for forty litres of petrol, that sort of thing . . . Emma was fairly black and white at the beginning, headstrong, tough, no bullshit. There wasn't a lot of femininity about her – that came after she had been there for a while and they decided they needed to soften her up. All of a sudden you'd see her in a dress and people would say, "Oh, she looks all right! That was nice, I liked that." '

Romance was inevitable, on-screen romance, that is. In no time at all the writers had Emma married to Sam Patterson, played by Peter O'Brien, working on the proven theory that there is nothing like a wedding to help ratings. Weddings are to soapies, or drama series, as car chases are to cop shows. If viewers are displaying disloyal tendencies, such as tuning in to another programme, a wedding will bring them back, hopefully for good. The only unfortunate thing about the romance between Emma and Sam was that some London newspapers, now hopelessly besotted by Australian soapie actors, confused it with the actors' private lives. Peter was then involved with Elaine Smith, of *Neighbours*, prompting one newspaper reporter to gush:

'Peter is torn between two star lovers. He still loves Elaine, but he's desperately attracted to Rebecca. It isn't all over between him and Elaine, but he's spending a lot of time with Rebecca.'

After recovering from a fit of laughter, Rebecca's reply was simple: 'He's not my type – and I don't suppose I'm his, either. . .'

Her popularity brought another problem, not uncommon to actresses. Olivia Newton-John has faced it. So has Jodie Foster. They have become the subject of a fan's obsession. Not a harmless obsession, it should be pointed out, but one that can be dangerous. In Rebecca's case it was a man who believed he was the Son of God and Rebecca his virgin bride. 'He's driving me out of my mind,' Rebecca told *TV Week*.

The victim of more than enough press gossip and half-truths, Rebecca Gibney's saving grace is her steadfast Christian faith

She first became aware of the man when still in New Zealand. He would write her strange letters, explaining his exalted position and inquiring when Rebecca would be ready to slip into the bridal gown. When she moved to Australia, he followed and continued with the same annoying, at times frightening, nonsense.

Then she was terrorised by a prowler, who may or may not have been the same person. Sitting in the lounge of her Melbourne terrace home one night, enjoying a glass of red wine and a book, she heard a scratching at the window. She ignored it. Maybe it was just a branch. Then came a sound like a long-drawn-out *ssshhh*. She turned and at the window was the figure of a man. Terrified, she leapt to her feet and ran to the door. But the man had disappeared. He came back again and again, creeping up to the window at night and emitting the curious, hair-raising *ssshhh* sound. It played havoc with Rebecca's nerves until she thought out the matter and decided a dog was a girl's best friend:

'I thought, to hell with this. Just because I'm female, somebody out there thinks he can terrorise me. But he's wrong. So I went out and got myself a bull terrier, which I've still got, and I don't mind being at home on my own now. I've also learnt some self-defence.'

After this trauma, her private life went smoothly for a while. She became engaged to Scott Rawlings, a sound technician and a wedding date was set. 'I can't complain at all,' she said.

Then her life changed. Perhaps the Great Planner thought she was having too much fun. For reasons she will not discuss, she broke it off with Scott. It was then she returned to the beliefs of her childhood, back to Christianity. 'It has changed my life,' she told reporter Christopher Day. 'It has given me new meaning, something to believe in. It has given me peace.'

Actually, her Christian upbringing had never deserted her. It was always there but had been pushed into the background as she had been discovering life. She began thinking of the spiritual side when her brother, Patrick, developed a brain tumour. He was twenty-three and his wife was expecting their first child. The doctors looked at him and shook their heads. He would die. If he didn't die he would be paralysed. An operation was his only hope but the doctors told the family to prepare for the worst.

'But Patrick had this incredible faith,' said Rebecca. 'I found people who didn't even know him were praying for him. Three days after the operation he was sitting up in bed. The doctors were amazed. They couldn't explain it.'

His faith inspired her. So did that of her three sisters who, one by one, became Christians. She saw the changes in their lives, the aura of peace and happiness which always seem to surround them. She was convinced that life had to be lived as a Christian.

'My childhood faith was rekindled,' she said. 'People say it's a cop-out. It isn't. You just let go of all the bad things. You turn the negative into positive. It's a really nice way to live. I don't call myself religious or a born again Christian. I am simply Christian. I have a definite belief in God and Jesus Christ. I am certainly not perfect . . . I am not a Bible basher but it is the way I choose to finish one week and start the next. I'll tell you this, I've never been happier in my life.'

MAURIE AND MAX

Eels! They were everywhere – long ones, short ones, wriggly ones, floppy ones – all of them slippery and squirmy and all of them very much alive when they should have been dead!

'The bloody things are alive!' yelled Maurie from the middle of the stream. 'You said they'd be dead!'

He swung on Max Cullen, swaying beside him and making strangling noises. 'What are you laughing at, you mug?'

Before Max could say a word, his face went white and his body stiffened.

'There's one in me pocket,' he said hoarsely. And it was Maurie's turn to laugh.

And that was how two of Australia's most famous character actors began their famous 'Battle of the Eels' for an episode of *The Flying Doctors*. It was supposed to be a simple story about publican Vic Buckley (Maurie) giving garage mechanic 'Hurtle' Morrison (Max) a lesson in eel catching, but it turned out to be a lesson in Murphy's Law; everything that could go wrong did go wrong and actors and film crew dissolved into chaos. This is how it happened:

It was after dark at Coopers Crossing (Minyip) and, as usual, freezing cold. The last water scene, when Liz Burch and Andrew McFarlane were attacked in a dam by small, hungry yabbies, had cost hours in precious production time and the director prayed nothing would go wrong this time. The problem potential was much higher the second time around. The script called for Maurie to show Max the intricacies of catching eels. The stream had long been fished out, so the locals said, and one of the prop men had been despatched to the Melbourne fish markets for a couple of buckets of the slippery serpents. The idea was to empty them upstream so Max and Maurie could pluck them triumphantly from the water as they slid past. That was the idea.

Though they loved the bush for its pubs (especially the pubs), the people and the gum trees, Max and Maurie were very much city blokes and preferred their eels in creeks, where they belonged. The idea of actually grappling with one of the slimy creatures was something akin to hopping into a nest full of taipans. Catching dead eels was marginally better, but still pretty awful. What they should have done, like any sensible researchers, was to go to the local kids and ask them if there were any eels left in the creek. Such an obvious and mundane approach is below the dignity of big time research teams.

So Max and Maurie splashed into the centre of the creek. They were protected from the icy water by thigh-length wading boots, although, again somebody had failed to do their homework and by the time Max reached midstream he realised there was a large hole in one of the boots and not only was his right leg suddenly encased in a block of ice but the combination of the extra weight and the soft muddy bottom had virtually anchored him into the middle of the stream.

'OK, give us some light,' called the director and with hisses and pops the scene was bathed in a glare of arc lamps. A faint voice was heard upstream:

'Will I chuck 'em in now?'

'Go for your life,' yelled the director and Max and Maurie started scooping the water with nets and saying what the script called them to say. There were a couple of splashes upstream and Max looked up expectantly, as one espying distant eels.

'I thought you said they were dead,' he shouted.

'Of course they're bloody dead,' the director shouted back. 'You try sitting in a freezer for a couple of weeks and see how lively you end up.'

'I still can't see the bloody things,' yelled Max, mollified.

'Use your net! Use your bloody net!'

Max and Maurie started bailing out the creek with their nets and were rewarded at last with a couple of long, slim, shiny hose-like objects which turned out to be eels. And, yes, quite dead. Definitely eels without feel.

'Got one!' yelled Maurie.

'Me too!' yelled Max and they both dipped the nets in for another go. That's when it happened.

As Maurie's net came up he saw an eel that was quite definitely unthawed. This was an eel with plenty of feel, thrashing and wriggling all over the place and threatening to fly out of the net and doubtless sink its teeth into his throat. Not only that, he could feel the creatures squirming in the stream below him. Pictures of sea monsters dragging him into the bitter depths flashed through his mind. Eels, like spiders, have a funny place in the human imagination.

'The bloody place is alive with the bastards!' yelled Maurie and he ploughed towards the bank like a paddle steamer, thrashing and swearing at anything and everything.

'Wait for me,' yelled Max, panic-stricken at being left all alone in a stream of squirming sea monsters. The rest of the crew were no help. They were toppling amongst the lights and cameras shrieking with laughter and showing no signs of sympathy whatsoever. Max swore and turned to follow Maurie. That was when he discovered he couldn't move. The weight of the water-filled wading boot had firmly anchored his leg in the soft mud and struggle as he might, it just wouldn't budge. Then, horror of horrors, one of the eels discovered the hole in his wader, doubtless under the impression that this was a nice little cave to hide in until the mad beast above him stopped thrashing about and turning the quiet stream into a maelstrom. It popped in and started curling around Max's leg for a bit of warmth.

'Holy shit!' shrieked Max. 'I've got one in my pocket.'

This was too much. Maurie, white-faced and panting as he reached the shore, just collapsed in a choking heap. So did everyone else. Max, firmly anchored in midstream, spent the next five minutes hooting and roaring and threatening all sorts of horrible retribution on the film crew, Maurie, the eels and even the arc lamps. Eventually someone threw him a rope and Max managed to winch himself ashore. They peeled off their soaking clothes and squatted there slowly going blue with cold while the director kept telling them to 'think hot!'

'Hot my arse,' yelled Maurie and joined Max in cursing the cold, cursing the director, cursing the Flying Doctor and most of all cursing the half-wit who decided there were no eels in the stream. Of course what nobody realised at the time was that most Australian inland streams have eels and can never be fished out because they do their spawning at sea and re-stock every year. You'd never know they were there, because they've become quite wary of humans over the years, but any bush kid will tell you all you need is a hook on the end of a long stick and a full moon. And there lay the answer. What got them all excited and rushing out of their holes in a feeding frenzy were the bright lights suddenly illuminating the dark. Like the world's biggest full moon.

Maurie, a great raconteur in a land that breeds them by the bucket-load, told the story over a beer and added:

'I was down at the creek a couple of days later and this city bloke arrived in a Landrover and asked one of the locals if he could drive across.

'"No problems," said the local.

'The city bloke took a good look at the creek again. It was still flowing pretty fast, and said, "You sure it's not too deep?"

'"No problems," said the local.

'"How can you tell?" asked the city bloke.

'"No problems," said the local. "It only comes half way up on me ducks."'

Maurie cackled to himself.

'He probably ended up like I did. Eel-hauled.'

The much-loved and well-respected Maurie Fields plays Vic Buckley, the Coopers Crossing publican

Although the Max and Maurie team split up when Max quit the series, the main team, Maurie and his wife Val Jallay, remain its most enduring old troupers. But their partnership goes back a lot further. Last year they celebrated their thirtieth wedding anniversary, something of a record in the topsy-turvy world of show business, where marriages usually last until the next script. But after three decades of doing everything from vaudeville to *The Flying Doctors*, everyone agreed they were as much in love as ever.

Val first laid eyes on Maurie thirty-seven years ago. She was a producer with Sorlies Revue Company and Maurie auditioned with his 'Skit and Skat' comedy duo. Born into a travelling vaudeville family, he'd been in show business since the age of six when he made a stage appearance with his mother doing vaudeville, cabaret, pantomimes, musical comedies, drama, radio, television, movies – anything and everything that came along.

'When we met he was wearing a zoot suit, a red hat, red shoes and a blacked face,' Val later told *Woman's Day* reporter Suzanne Monks. 'I thought his music was great . . . but, oh my, his jokes were bad! They've improved a lot since, I might add. We all used to go to the pub after the show. If there was a piano, Maurie would sit down and tinkle away and sing the blues.

'I was fascinated by those clever fingers. Then one day I thought, "You're not such a bad sort of fellow." I took a good look at him and thought, "You've got blue eyes and a nice smile. You're not bad looking." Best of all, he was gentle and kind and so shy. Absolutely the shyest person I had met. I think I might just have changed that.'

Maurie had long fancied Val from a distance and they started courting, in the true old-fashioned sense of the word. Val said she'd be lucky to get a peck on the cheek when he took her out. He proposed one starry, moonlit night on a deserted beach and they've been inseparable ever since – on and off stage – often appearing in double acts on stage together and separately in television appearances. For the past six years they have been the popular Coopers Crossing publicans, Vic and Nancy Buckley.

One of Australia's most sought-after actors, Maurie managed to squeeze in *The Flying Doctors* between other jobs. 'As a mini-series role it didn't take up a great deal of time. But after it went to air they came along and said the response was so good that they were planning to turn it into a regular series and would Val and I be interested. Apparently the pub role had been written specifically with me in mind. Well, we've been there ever since, in charge of the pub.' It was a perfect piece of type-casting – in more ways than one. Maurie, a noted elbow bender, has only to walk through a pub door to make it look real. A couple of years ago he suffered a severe heart attack and had to drastically

Max Cullen plays garage
mechanic Hurtle Morrison

change his life-style – he was only allowed to drink light ale.

'I'm on the .09 (light beer), three a day. When I got the news it was the worst twenty minutes of my life. Apart from cutting out the beer, I had to cut out cigarettes, I had to cut out sex. Now I cut out paper dolls.'

It's no great shakes for a publican with his fondness for the foaming brown. To Maurie, drinking is a culture, a way of life. Fifteen years ago he set up a Beer Drinkers' Protection Society in Victoria after seven rises in the price of beer in a single year: 'We have to stop the dog chasing its tail or we'll all go broke. We have already got 600 members and we are going to petition the government and politicians. Beer is our national drink. You can't drink water – fish fornicate in it.'

Although one of the country's best known actors, Maurie never scored a starring role. Not that he minded. 'Never be the bloody star because when you're doing a show and assisting, if it all goes well, you can walk up to the lead and say: "Hey, we killed 'em didn't we?" If it doesn't work, you can do the same thing – walk up and say: "Gee, what happened to you?" '

His broad Australian accent proved a handicap in the old days. He once told Jenny Brown of the *Melbourne Age*:

'I always reckoned it wasn't that I was too Australian, everyone else was too Pommified. They used to plum on through their lines and I'd say, "Howzat? Can you slip that one to me again?" These days it's different, of course; now they need me for the resident mongrel. Not that I'm doing Ocker. I hate Ocker. [The term applies to over-emphasising the worst aspects of the Australian no-hoper.] I base my characters on people I've met, especially country people, who are real. There are so many different types that you could play on forever without running out. Those dead-set, fair dinkum people who would give you their last dina. They're Aussies and I'm Aussie.'

If Maurie was typecast as a bush publican, there's some of Hurtle Morrison, the Coopers Creek garage mechanic, in Max Cullen. Like Hurtle, Max could never pass up a chance to make a spare quid and after his stint on *The Flying Doctors* he thought he'd have a go at movie production, mainly because he'd bought the screen rights to David Williamson's successful play, *Sons of Cain*, for a bottle of French champagne!

'The most I've ever paid for film rights,' he grumbled at the time. 'My first movie only cost a dollar.'

A dry chap, Max – with or without champagne.

The movie coup of the decade followed a chance remark by Williamson's agent that *Sons of Cain* was his only play not yet on film.

'How much for the screen rights?' quipped Max, about as financially equipped to buy movies as launch a raid on the Bank of England. Neither was to know Williamson had been so impressed with Max's stage role as the hard-nosed reporter Kevin Cassidy that he had decided to give him a break.

'Tell Lettuce Face he's up for fifty bucks or a bottle of Bollinger,' said the playwright. (During the play's triumphant London season, a critic likened Max's face to a 'frenzied lettuce'. Bollinger was the champagne consumed so copiously in the play.)

'Done!' said Max and set about raising the finance, his backers doubtless hoping real life Max would make a better fist of things than the time Hurtle Morrison went into the home-brewing business and nearly poisoned half the population of Coopers Crossing!

The movie is plodding ahead but in the meantime he's planning to return to London late this year with a new production of Ray Lawler's Australian classic, *Summer of the Seventeenth Doll*. He'll be doing one of the two male leads as Barney, the sugar-cane cutter first played by Lawler himself and made internationally famous by John Mills in the movie version. It will be Max's third London stage appearance; the second was another Williamson play, *Emerald City*, in which he played Mike the conman.

Val Jallay and Maurie Fields who play Nancy and Vic Buckley in the series. As much in love as ever they have already celebrated over thirty years together in show business

Leading journalist Terry Blake once described Max as a limelighter who hated the limelight – one of Australia's most seen and least known celebrities, from Hurtle Morrison to Chooka the Pom-stirring reporter in *Bodyline* (the highly successful mini-series about the 1931/32 England Ashes tour of Australia when Douglas Jardine's infamous 'leg theory' tactics combined with fast bowler Harold Larwood's deadly bouncers almost led to a breakdown in relations between the two countries).

They broke the mould with Max. Jack Nicholson perfected the manic eyes, Paul Hogan the dangerous grin. Max invented the quizzical grimace. His thinking was described as neither lateral nor vertical; it was everywhere. Having a conversation with him was hard work.

105

'Nice day, isn't it?' asked Blake.

By the time he'd tortured his way through the remark's inherent complexities, identified the pitfalls, lit his eyes with revelation and said:

'Yeah.'

Blake was looking around nervously for the door.

An actor by whim as much as talent, Max also tried his hand at painting, cartooning, writing, directing, sculpting and music. He hated being interviewed. Apart from the intrusion, he had to come up with an answer. Usually, in what passed for 'normal' conversation, he could grapple with all the convolutions of a question until quizzical grimacing scared the questioner away or an association flickered on his mental screen. Then there'd be a disordered anecdote that might or might not provide an answer.

'Why did you leave *The Flying Doctors*?'

'Don't know. It was a good-looking series. Shot on film, plenty of scenery, laconic humour, odd-looking characters.'

'So why leave?'

'Yeah. I think I didn't want to do it any more. I think that's what the idea was.'

'You don't know why?'

'Yeah. I had a good idea why I didn't want to do any more. I'd had enough of it.'

'You're sure now?'

'Yeah. That's probably pretty close.'

He nodded, as one having explained Heisenberg's uncertainty principle to a pretty dumb carrot. Newspaper morgues don't have 'in-depth' interviews with Max Cullen.

Asked if he had any big names in mind for the movie, he said, with a deadpan look on his face:

'How about Rebecca Gibney as the young inexperienced journalist?'

Had she been approached?

'No.'

Why not?

'She wouldn't be right for the part.'

A desperate change of tack. Did he ever get stagefright?

'Never. When I'm on stage I know exactly what I've got to say next.

Max Cullen in the Australian film *Sunday Too Far Away*

It's a lot better than real life. I used to write ad-libs on the back of my hand so if I ran into someone on the street I'd have something to say. The worst thing about being on stage is forgetting your lines. Life, too.'

The man's agonising shyness could have anchored him in agoraphobia. Instead, he went about as public as you could get. Not sure which art would lead to his soul, he tried the lot. A true craftsman who couldn't make up his mind which craft to be true to, Max became one of the top ten Australian actors; a reluctant darling of the theatrical set when he'd much prefer the following description by a colleague:

'This bloke's not some slack-jawed retard from the Coke commercial beefstakes. This bloke's an actor's actor. He does his homework and doesn't stuff about. He brings paper people to life. You ever see a bigger bastard than that Quinn in *Act of Betrayal*? He's a bloody genius to work with. He's forgotten more than most of us will ever learn.'

Well, there's no bitterness like show bitterness but Max would rather talk about the music teacher who taught him trumpet at the age of seventeen. 'Man, you're a natural,' said the teacher. Thirty years later Max went back and his old tutor recognised him. Far out, thought Max,

107

after all those years. Next day the teacher said, 'Now I know where I remember you from. You play Hurtle in *The Flying Doctors*.'

Some of Max's feature film credits include Gillian Armstrong's *My Brilliant Career* and *Starstruck*, John Duigan's *Dimboola* and *Sunday Too Far Away*, Tom Jeffrey's *The Odd Angry Shot*, Claude Whatham's *Hoodwink*, Stephen Wallace's *Stir*, Quentin Masters' *Midnite Spares*, and *Boundaries of the Heart* with Wendy Hughes.

Among his television work are the mini-series *The Scales of Justice*, *The Eureka Stockade*, *Act of Betrayal* with Elliott Gould, and the series *Rafferty's Rules*, *A Country Practice* and, of course, *The Flying Doctors*.

The Flying Doctors was something of a watershed in Max's life. It led to a divorce from his second wife, actress Colleen Fitzpatrick, after fourteen years. Then media pressure killed off any chance of a relationship with co-star Liz Burch becoming more serious. The split with Colleen came just after they'd finished doing up their 140-year-old stone cottage in Sydney. Max's comments were typical of him:

'The only way you know you have a future is to leave a thing unfinished. If the renovations hadn't been completed I'd still be laying bricks, and, I suppose, we'd still be together. Now there's no going back. All the mortar is in place.'

Then came the romance with Liz.

'There was nothing deep between us, ever. I know it makes good copy, but we're just good friends. The press hounded us for a while and I think that's what finished us off. It became too public. We decided to call it a day. If it had been serious, there would have been hell to pay from Liz' parents because I was still married. I still like her a lot. She's very attractive and intelligent. A good catch for any man who isn't boring, married or gay.'

Or an offbeat, brilliant actor.

But then *The Flying Doctors* always attracted the best of Australian talent – amongst them Lenore Smith as Sister Kate Wellings, Pat Evison as Violet Carnegie, Bruce Barry as George Baxter and Terry Gill as Sgt Carruthers. They're not the supernovae, but they're the back-bone of a series like this, the no-nonsense, highly experienced professionals who never miss a beat; the ones that the beginners come to for advice after their first nerve-racking day on the set.

THE OTHER COOPERS CROSSING REGULARS

The champagne was flowing at the opening night of Andrew Lloyd Webber's *Cats* in Sydney, when a voice over loudspeakers suddenly ordered everyone out of the building. 'Someone's planted a bomb in the theatre,' said the voice. 'Everyone outside, quickly!'

Lenore Smith was in the first night crowd, but with the true unruffled calm she displays as Sister Kate Wellings in *The Flying Doctors*, she strolled casually into the street without spilling a drop of champagne. That was when she spotted an old friend, actor Matt Kay, wandering down George Street looking at her curiously.

'What's going on?' he asked.

'Nothing really,' said Lenore. '*Cats* is about to bomb. Would you like to come and watch?'

With that she took the astonished actor by the arm and led him back into the foyer where the party was going full swing. Instead of a bomb going off, a fuse was lit between Lenore and Matt. Two days later they moved in together and a few weeks after that they got married. It was a side of Lenore Smith you'd never see in Kate Wellings.

Cats didn't bomb, but the marriage did. Last year Matt and Lenore announced their separation, making it failed marriage number two for Lenore (her first was to Gary Sweet, who played Donald Bradman in *Bodyline*), a state of affairs that would be looked on with horror by cautious Kate. As a colleague commented: 'If Lenore Smith lived at the North Pole and Sister Kate Wellings lived at the South Pole, you'd be getting an idea of how far apart the two characters are.'

Lenore was born and bred in the inner Sydney suburb of Balmain, a one-time tough, working-class district now domiciled by Yuppies, real estate speculators, artists, writers and actors. Her bubbly, chatty, outgoing personality has to be held tightly in check when she plays country girl Kate, the dedicated flying nurse with a relaxed, easygoing nature. Kate is not a big talker. Lenore is.

'As a Balmain girl, I have to be careful not to inject too much pace into the role. Everything has to be slowed down to about a tenth of my city speed so things move along at the accepted rate in Coopers Crossing.'

Indeed, life was very straightforward and predictable for Sister Kate until citified Dr Geoff Standish (Robert Grubb) replaced Dr Tom Callaghan (Andrew McFarlane) in the main role. Kate spent most of the time torn between her attraction towards him and the fear of becoming romantically involved. That all came to an end when they finally realised they were 'made for each other' in true soapie style and after a roller-coaster romance, ended up at the altar. It didn't do the ratings any harm, although Lenore insists it wasn't a gimmick:

'We played a significant part in developing the characters to the point where they'd be married. We were forever pestering the producers, giving them guidelines. We certainly wouldn't have done it just to chase ratings. In fact, they told us that once we were married on television we'd be dead meat. It hasn't developed that way. It's a great challenge because in my past television, movie and stage work I've never been seen as the romantic type.'

Crawford's Chief Executive Officer, Terry Ohlsson, pointed out there was never any doubt about the viewing public's acceptance of the romance: 'People don't realise it, but every letter they write to us is read and the good ideas often acted upon. For many viewers, the crowd at Coopers Crossing is almost a second family. There are adults out there who've followed the series since they were teenagers. If they hadn't liked what we were doing, they'd have told us about it pretty smartly, I can assure you of that. Sometimes people start their

Lenore Smith plays the efficient and hard-headed Sister Kate Wellings, who is finally won over by her colleague Dr Geoff Standish

letters with lines like, "I know you'll never take any notice of what I'm about to say, but . . ." Well, they couldn't be more wrong. They're our family too, and if someone takes the trouble of writing when they think their letter's not even going to be read, then they're the ones who obviously care a lot. You'd be astounded at the amount of mail we get from England, Holland and Belgium. Let's face it, *The Flying Doctors* has been playing overseas a lot longer than *Neighbours* or *Home and Away* and while our audience may not be quite as big, we're solid and in there for the long haul.

'At one stage, the producers of Holland's biggest television sitcom were going to shoot a couple of episodes in Australia and then maroon the family in the outback and have the Flying Doctor come to rescue them. It fell through because of impossible time schedules, but it will give you an idea of how big we are in Europe and how seriously we take our task. If two brilliant actors like Lenore and Robert think it's what we should do, and we get the right feed-back from our viewing "family" then that's what we do.'

Lenore hasn't had the same success in her real-life marriages, possibly because she doesn't put as much homework into them as she does on screen. Her 'instant-bliss' marriage to Matt Kay was almost a carbon copy of her first failed attempt with Gary Sweet. They met by the lift at Crawford Productions. At the time he was playing Magpie in *The Sullivans* and Lenore had finished a stint with *The Restless Years*. An absolute stunner, she was first refused the role of the seventeen-year-old schoolgirl Diane Archer, because the producer and casting director thought she was too beautiful. Gary Sweet had no such reservations.

'I'd just finished doing a voice-over when I saw Lenore standing near the lift in this terrible raincoat. It was the worst thing I'd ever seen in my life . . . but the wearer looked absolutely gorgeous. I said something corny like, "Haven't I seen you somewhere before?" In actual fact I'd never seen her on television, but I knew her face because of all the publicity. She didn't know me at all, which was a blow to my ego. We got into the lift and by the time we reached the ground floor we had a date for lunch. We were engaged three weeks later.'

Lenore, in strictly non-Sister Kate style, said it was a case of love at first sight. 'We seemed to chat all the time. We had similar backgrounds, we liked the same authors and we shared a similar sense of humour.' They were married a couple of months later in the sunlit, ivy-walled garden of Gary's parents' home in Adelaide, only to split up soon afterwards. 'It ended pretty quickly,' was Lenore's brief, and only public comment.

Her second marriage lasted five years until an equally brief statement was issued: 'Matt and I have agreed to separate. We are still close friends and we won't comment further.' Perhaps a make-believe television marriage is what Lenore really wants. Certainly her life is devoted to the screen, big and little. Co-star Robert believes she is one of the most talented and dedicated actors around. 'Lenore is a highly intelligent, extremely inventive person. She's absolutely marvellous to work with in *The Flying Doctors*. We can spend hours working our way through plot ideas and character development. She really knows her job. She could become anything if she puts her mind to it. I personally believe she'll end up directing movies in a few years. She's really that good.'

Lenore did two and a half years training with Sydney's prestigious Ensemble Theatre before joining the cast of *The Restless Years*, a soapie that pre-dated *Neighbours* but showed a curious Australian talent for producing television series like sausages. She also appeared in major Australian series such as *Cop Shop*, *The Young Doctors*, and *The Sullivans*.

Whereas Lenore's television role is in direct contrast to her own life, Pat Evison, as the matriarch of Coopers Crossing, is almost an example of nature imitating art. At one stage the producers decided a nice sub-plot would entail Violet discovering she had diabetes. At her next medical check-up, Pat was diagnosed as a non-insulin dependent diabetic. Not long ago she was written out of the series on the pretext that she wanted to spend time with her family overseas and look after her grandson. In fact, Pat left the show because she wanted to spend time with her family overseas and look after her grandchildren!

'I'd planned to spend a couple of months with my daughter and her husband in France and get to know their children better. It was all arranged and then my holidays were cut short because Channel Nine wanted me back earlier. As far as I was concerned, it wasn't on. I simply refused to mess my family around like that.'

Pat Evison as Violet Carnegie, the matriarch and gossip of Coopers Crossing, here in a scene from the series with former Flying Doctor, Andrew McFarlane

New Zealand-born Pat could afford to take a lofty view. Her impeccable theatrical credentials ensured she'd never be out of work. She trained at London's Old Vic Centre as a director and was one of only four students selected for the advanced production course. She's long been recognised as a major talent in all aspects of theatre and tutored both New Zealand's Opera Company and Ballet Company. In 1980 she was awarded the O.B.E. for services to New Zealand Theatre. She went to Australia to do a one-woman show, *An Evening With Katherine Mansfield* at Sydney's upper crust Old Tote theatre and graduated to television with *Matlock, Division Four, A Town Like Alice* and *Prisoner*. Her movies include *Caddie, Tim, The Earthling* and *Starstruck*. Down-to-earth and outspoken, she once said she was brought up to believe that: 'If you had talent you shouldn't hide it under a bushel, and I've got a very large bushel.'

As the lovable, gossipy grandmother, and eventually great grandmother in *The Flying Doctors*, she knows everybody within a radius of

100 miles of Coopers Crossing. Offstage is a different story. The trouble began when she failed to recognise a couple of well-known actors – mainly because they'd never been screened in New Zealand. Her biggest *faux pas*, she told *Woman's Day* reporter, Heather Waby, was not knowing who Maurie Fields was when she met him for the first time at Minyip:

'I'd done a scene with his wife Val and she told me her husband was coming up next day. I thought he'd be someone like my own husband and said how nice it was for him to come up and join Val on the set. When Maurie arrived, Val asked me to join them for drinks and dinner. I asked Maurie if he was an actor and he gave me this very strange look and said "Yes" and left it at that. Val didn't say anything so I thought he must be an extra. At dinner, people rushed over for his autograph. I felt about the size of a pea when I realised how famous he was. I'd just never seen him in New Zealand.'

A well-trained and well-respected actress, Pat Evison has rarely found herself out of work. Here with Mel Gibson in the film *Tim*

Pat did it again at the Logies Awards, Australia's own version of the Emmys but much more enjoyable because of the generous amount of booze laid on. The place was full of famous stars, many of whom she did recognise. She was ushered to a table and introduced herself, as New Zealanders are wont, to someone she'd never seen before. He said his name was Reg Grundy and because he didn't look or behave like one of the 'beautiful people' she asked him what 'he did for a crust'. His reaction was similar to Maurie's and Pat knew she'd put her foot in it again. Grundy Productions, as it happened, ranked with Crawford Productions as one of Australia's biggest television production houses and responsible, among other things, for *Neighbours*. It was rather like asking Cecil B. De Mille if he was in the movie business.

This August, Pat and her husband will celebrate their forty-third year of wedded bliss together – or perhaps apart would be more accurate. However, unlike Lenore, their separations are not permanent. Pat realised early in her marriage that if she was going to make a success of the theatre, she'd have to move to greener pastures than New Zealand. But she also decided it would be more realistic to hop on a plane for regular visits to husband Roger, a consultant civil engineer, than ask him to sacrifice his business on the risky premise of her making it big in show business. These days, it's a regular occurrence to take off for New Zealand when she has a few days break. With her eldest son, John, living in Canada and daughter, Anne, in France, it's quite an international family.

If Bruce Barry had had his way, *The Flying Doctors* would have gone well and truly international; at one stage he was negotiating to have Joan Collins come to Australia to play 'superbitch' to his *Flying Doctors* version of J. R. Ewing in *Dallas*.

Bruce played the rich, obnoxious grazier George Baxter who thought he could run Coopers Crossing because he owned most of the land around the town – or did until selling out to an American consortium. That was when the Joan Collins idea came in.

'What we needed was a resident superbitch to head a dynasty based on a trans-Pacific company set up in Coopers Crossing. She would have to be mean enough to match Baxter's bastardry but have a lot of charm and persuasion. I thought Joan was ideal for the role, but failing that, Linda Kowolski would have done just nicely. She has a lovely blend of wit, sensuality and charm.' He admitted he never did get to talk it over with Linda's husband (then boyfriend) Australian megastar Paul Hogan. Joan Collins also gave him a polite thumbs down, so he had to settle for being Australia's favourite television baddie all on his own.

Bruce makes no secret of his debt to J.R. of *Dallas*. He once said he based thirty per cent of the role on J.R., another thirty per cent on himself and forty per cent on Malcolm Fraser, Australia's last conservative Prime Minister and a man of stony visage and strong, if not popular views.

'I feel I'm doing a public service by making viewers antagonistic towards a character like George. I always think that if you can present the darker side of society on the screen, then people can see things more objectively and learn more about life. Mind you, George is not totally objectionable and in many ways is a highly responsible and desirable chap. However, he does get overbearing and self-righteous at times.'

As one of Australian television's leading matinee idols, the 'bad guy' role came as a shock to most viewers. His rugged good looks and smooth delivery had always brought him plum 'nice guy' parts in such series as *Skyways*, *The Spoiler*, *Bellbird*, *The Restless Years* and *Motel*. He also has a fine singing voice and got his big chance on London's West End stage in 1977 with *The Biograph Girl*, a musical about the early days of Hollywood based on the career of director D. W. Griffith, played by Barry. He was understandably bitter when it folded after six weeks and let loose a broadside at the British theatre that was closer to a J.R. tantrum than the level-headed response of a cool professional.

'It's the British tradition of pantomime transvestites that made it flop. If they didn't camp around with girls dressed as boys, critics might not reach for their guns every time they heard an overture to a British musical.' Having got that off his chest, he went on to have a fairly successful stint in England, including the role of journalist John Wagner in Tom Stoppard's *Night and Day*, before returning to Sydney and once again 'having Bondi Beach on tap' – as he puts it.

Born in Gympie, Queensland, and reared in the outback shearing town of Charters Towers, his outback credentials for the George Baxter role were obvious. The whole family trained in musical

Bruce Barry as the
wealthy landowner,
George Baxter. Bruce
makes no secret of his
debt to J.R. with this role

instruments and voice production and he was a natural for local plays. After school he worked for a bank before realising there was more to life than sitting behind a tellers' cage counting other people's money. He hit the road selling encyclopaedias but had had enough by the time he got to Cairns, in far north Queensland, where he spent his last shilling on a beer. As it happened, tourism was starting to take off in the area and the publican was looking for a singing waiter.

'Look no further,' announced Bruce, who'd never served a table in his life. 'I'm Bruce Barry, the famous singing waiter of the outback.'

The publican eyed him doubtfully, but gave him a chance. It was his first taste of something close to professional theatre, and Bruce was hooked for life.

He went south to Brisbane and worked in radio drama for the ABC before trying his hand in the Sydney big time. He spent three years with the Young Elizabethan Players and ended up company leader before getting his first big break in the J. C. Williamson production of *Irma La Douce*, followed by twelve months with the Union Theatre in

Country cop Sergeant
Jack Carruthers is played
by Terry Gill. He has been
in almost every major
Australian television series

Melbourne. He says now that the prestige was fine but that the money was awful.

'I got married around that time and for the first few years Anne and I lived on Uncle Toby's Oats and milk. I suppose I'd do it again if I had to, but baby, there's no satisfaction on the breadline. Believe me, an artist doesn't do his best work when he's starving in a garret. For ten years I was in debt, borrowing from mothers, fathers, sisters and brothers. The two children, Simone and Byron, were born during that period. The only clothes we had were on our backs. It was a real treat on Friday night to buy a flagon of really rough red.'

It's a bit different these days. Bruce spends a lot of his time landscaping the huge garden in his rambling old home at Hunters Hill, a Sydney Harbour waterfront suburb. He says it's a back to nature thing, a trait that might sit comfortably with George Baxter, but certainly not J. R. Ewing. In fact, apart from being an avid conservationist, Bruce Barry is a deep thinking, highly committed man. In a letter to the national daily *The Australian*, he spelt out his thoughts on the problems facing the country. It read, in part:

'There's no doubt we're a savagely materialistic society – an unwitting answer to our national inferiority complex. If you don't have breeding, tradition and culture, you make up for it with wool, minerals and money. No matter that we're a nation of untold wealth, this inferiority complex will persist while we crave the cultures and traditions of other people. The English, the French and the Americans all have their inferiority complexes and they're not going to let up pressuring us into ours. Unfortunately, all but the wisest top dogs believe they can remain top dog only by keeping the underdog under.

'But mankind is mellowing, particularly our youth. More and more we're realising our true histories are written in the arts. We remember the Greeks for their philosophers, the Romans for their painters, sculptors and musicians. And though he was a power only yesterday, we remember France not for de Gaulle but for Balzac, Rodin, Sartre and Yves St Laurent. Perhaps we remember Germany for Hitler, but the enduring influences of that great country will be the Goethes and the Beethovens.'

So much for the shallow matinee idol. And the tough guy image? Well, there's no doubt he looks the part – but it's all an act.

At school, in Charters Towers, many years ago, one of his best friends got into a fight with the local bully.

'Lay off him,' ordered Bruce. 'Or I'll hammer you one myself.'

The bully stopped and looked his new opponent up and down. Bruce had never been pushy in the past and the bully was smart enough to realise that the quiet ones were often the most dangerous. Especially when they were as big as Bruce.

'What's it got to do with you?' he asked, sticking his chin out.

By now thoroughly committed, Bruce had to stick his own chin out in response and they stood there, hands on hips, eyeball to eyeball. Bruce's mate, seeing his opportunity, let loose a roundhouse left at the bully, who ducked just in time, leaving the way open for the flying fist to connect with Bruce's chin. *Bang*! It was a good punch and Bruce was flat on his back. A teacher arrived at that moment and they carted Bruce off to the sick bay. His heroics had earned him a dislocated jaw!

'That was my first and last fight,' said Bruce ruefully. 'Now I just look menacing and hope they'll go away.'

Obviously a man of many parts, but perhaps not as many as co-star Terry Gill, who once spent a couple of weeks combining his no-nonsense country cop role of Sergeant Jack Carruthers (Terry's an ex-police cadet) with that of a low-life drug-runner in an episode of *Mission Impossible* (an American series made in Australia), while spending nights sending up everything from suburban ballet schools to Australian rock star Johnny Farnham at his Melbourne theatre restaurant. He once appeared on three different channels in one week – *The Sullivans*, *Prisoner* and *Skyways* – while performing children's pantomimes during the day in suburban shopping centres. It's all part of a life of endless confusion for a wandering Cornishman who went from being a fatherless American/Celt to Jewish orphan while rearing one of Australia's leading show business families.

'I'd always thought my father was a World War II American soldier who married my mother and later separated. But during a holiday back in my home town of Truro, in Cornwall, I learnt my dad was actually a Russian Jew who travelled around selling jewellery and has since died. I thought, "I've gone to bed Celtic and woken up Jewish!" Still, at least I now know where I came from.'

Where he's come is a long way from doing repertory in England, although he did appear with Susan Hampshire in a West End production of *Past Imperfect*. Since coming to Australia with his English bride, actress Carole Anne Aylett, in 1964, he's been in almost every major Australian television series including such prestigious productions as *Power Without Glory*, *I Can Jump Puddles* and *Water Under the Bridge*. Movies include *Crocodile Dundee* and *Phar Lap*.

He has some pretty strong views about children's television.

'The government should subsidise the commercial channels to produce decent kids shows. That's how *Sesame Street* got started in America. People wonder why kids come out of school and can't spell. It's because they sit and watch rubbish on television.'

A man of action as well as talk, Terry decided to do something about it and put together his own troupe of players to do children's pantomimes in shopping centres. He writes and produces them himself, with wife Carole working on scenery and costumes. The entire family treads the boards; Erin, twenty-one, is a dancer and musician. Edan, seventeen, is 'a bit of a worry'.

'In between shows he sits in his room all day listening to heavy metal rock and wearing black T-shirts with skulls on them. We throw him some raw meat every now and then and hope he'll come out to perform or ask for some money for a haircut. Not that it will do him any harm. I think it's a mistake today that young kids come into a soapie fresh from drama school. They often get big-headed from all the recognition and then disappear off the map. They lounge around and end up working in a coffee shop. At least Erin's getting some solid background in fronting live audiences. That's when we can lure him from his den, of course.'

Meanwhile, just in case they invent a twenty-five-hour day, Terry owns and runs the Bull 'n' Bush & Naughty Nineties theatre restaurant in Hawthorn, Melbourne. Life's a yawn.

REALISM

I f there's a single word to describe *The Flying Doctors'* knack of staying airborne in the tumult of wild whims and stormy ratings that rack the broadcasting firmaments, it is realism. From script-writer Terry Stapleton's reluctant, strife-ridden sojourn in outback Charleville to the rarefied heights of international success, the Crawford team never wavered in its determination to tell true stories about real people.

The temptation to turn it into some sort of outback *Mission Impossible* was resisted from the very first mini-series, and the show gained as a result. By playing down their extraordinary work and locations, Crawfords not only reflected the true attitude of the Flying Doctors but made the unbelievable believable. If you use hype and hoopla to tell a Manchester housewife about a place where doctors casually hop into aeroplanes to make house calls, she'll write it off as a poorly done *Monty Python*. Take it for granted, have everyone going about their daily affairs as if the bizarre was normal and the audience is far more likely to accept it. The BBC probably pioneered the approach decades ago with *Z Cars* which made an immense impact on Australian audiences. *The Flying Doctors* tells us what it's really like to perform emergency surgery miles from an operating theatre without Dr Kildare, or fly a light plane through a cyclonic depression without Mel Gibson. On occasions, however, it did become a little too real. . .

The twin-engined Navajo buzzed around the sky like a fly in a bottle as the pilot tried to shake loose the aircraft's jammed landing gear. On board, the eight passengers gripped their seats, bit their lips and tried not to throw up or scream with terror. All except one.

Actor Max Cullen looked curiously, first at his fellow passengers, mostly journalists, then through the window to the crazily pitching world outside. Finger to his lips, he studied the situation, taking in

every detail as a director would at a dress rehearsal. Only this was no
dress rehearsal. This was the real thing. The situation they'd filmed so
many times in the secure sound stage at Crawford Productions was
suddenly happening thousands of feet above Melbourne Airport.

The fifteen minutes of physical and mental anguish suddenly
became pure nightmare as Flight Captain Paton announced that the
undercarriage indicator still showed the wheels were jammed and
they were to brace themselves for an emergency landing. Reporter,
Janise Beaumont lowered her head between her knees as the person
next to her yelled: 'You can't do this. I haven't made a will!' Janise
admitted later than she didn't see the humour of the remark. She only
realised for the first time that she hadn't made a will either.

The aircraft straightened out and began its descent. The only sound
was the revving and slowing of the engines as the pilot adjusted air
speed and lowered the wing flaps. Sitting upright at his window seat,
Max surveyed the scene with renewed interest and lifted his portable
typewriter to his knee for safekeeping. Then it was time. The plane's
tailed dropped, the engines died to a whisper and all aboard braced
themselves for the thumping crash, the cartwheel, the explosion – and
fiery oblivion. Instead there was a slight jar of landing wheels, the
plane sped smoothly down the runway, the engines roared into reverse
and everyone straightened with a universal sigh of relief. Except Max.
He'd sat up and watched every detail. Now he was frowning slightly, as
if the performance had been a fizzer. He frowned even harder when he
stepped from the plane and his treasured typewriter fell to the tarmac
and broke into three pieces, one of them hitting the pilot's foot. They
were the only physical victims of the 'crash' landing, they and the faulty
landing gear indicator light.

With so much flying in the series, there were bound to be close
shaves. Most of them went unreported unless there were journalists
around. On another occasion a group of scribes were flying to
Horsham, the airport nearest Minyip, in a veteran DC3. Looking out of
the window, Sydney's *Daily Mirror* columnist, Gerri Sutton, saw
smoke pouring from one of the engines. This is it, she thought. She'd
spent her working life skylarking around the world in all sorts of
winged monsters, and now she was about to be wiped out in the plane
reputed to be the world's safest, right in her own backyard.

Again, the aircraft landed safely and everyone disembarked without a scratch. They boarded the bus for Minyip, and that's when reality became nature copying art. The genuine Flying Doctors often remarked that their real danger came, not from the planes they flew or the ploughed fields where they landed, but the earth-bound spitfire pilots who drove them from the airport to town. Time after time, RFDS crews have nearly come to grief at the hands of bush drivers intent on getting them from aircraft to patients in the shortest time possible, without regard to road conditions, curves or the maximum speed manageable in a clapped-out station-wagon, bus or truck.

In this case, having survived a potentially disastrous mid-air fire, the bus-load of reporters was nearly wiped out by a local fire engine roaring towards the airport to cope with the fire emergency. Said Gerri: 'We were just tooling along and counting our blessings when this bloody great fire engine careered up out of nowhere and nearly mowed us down in the middle of the road. Another two inches and all the Flying Doctors in the world couldn't have put us back together again.'

The on-screen realism soon led to *The Flying Doctors* taking on important social issues like AIDS and aboriginal welfare. The AIDS episode had the cutting edge of introducing debate about homosexuality into a small country town, and as a further bonus used macho *Division 4* star, Gerard Kennedy, as the Coopers Crossing war hero who comes home to die with his male lover of seventeen years.

Producer Oscar Whitbeard said they'd tried very hard to avoid sensationalism. 'It's a serious and tragic epidemic. Although we didn't set out to bombard the audience with detailed medical aspects of the disease, we definitely explored the social attitudes to male homosexuals in Australia. Many people won't like it because they hate homosexuals. "Poofter-bashing" is alive and well Down Under.'

Coopers Crossing is turned into a microcosm of bigotry towards homosexuality and sexually transmitted diseases. The town rejects their one-time hero and leaves him to die in an armchair. The locals at the pub even take to drinking out of cans and bottles rather than possibly 'contagious' glasses.

The episode drew mixed reaction from the critics. Some commended it for its head-on confrontation of the problem, the candid

Aboriginal actress, Kylie Belling, is Crawford Productions' answer to the problem of realistic aboriginal casting in the series. As young teenager Sharon Herbert, she soon becomes a regular face on our screens

dialogue and realistic incidents. Others said it left a general impression that the people of Coopers Crossing were 'sub-human' and there wasn't enough medical information when the programme was, after all, about doctors.

Bruce Best, producer of *A Country Practice*, sprang to the defence of his rivals: 'Earlier in the year we called in our researchers to write an AIDS episode, but decided medical evidence was changing so rapidly, we couldn't produce a definitive plot. Rather than simply cash in on the AIDS hysteria, we decided not to do it.'

Occasionally the scriptwriters do stray from the straight and narrow and dash off a bit of good old-fashioned whiz-bang fantasy – as Gerard Kennedy was to discover. Whether it was a reaction to his unlikely role as a homosexual or a subsequent appearance in *Mission Impossible*, Kennedy was invited back to play Luke Mitchell, a knockabout farrier from Queensland who comes skidding into town in a souped up panel van looking to do a bit of horse-shoeing. Hair unruly and muscles bulging from a sleeveless blue singlet, he's a far cry from the collar and tie television cop of old (or indeed real life ex-journalist who ploughs through physics, science and nature text books for a bit of light reading). He finds himself working part time for Vic and Val at the local pub and does it so well they offer him a job as manager. He's considering the idea when he gets blown up in a car. Dr Geoff Standish saves his life by putting him into a transcendental state and shutting down his body. As someone remarked at the time, 'The next thing you know, Shirley MacLaine will be doing a bit of astral travelling into the Crossing.'

The 'Aboriginal Problem', a delicate Australian euphemism for racial prejudice, was another issue they confronted – although Crawfords were uncharacteristically hamfisted about it at first. The plot called for an aboriginal woman to play the pivotal role of a land rights activist who arrives in town to help the local aborigines and ends up falling in love with a white man. A good, basic idea with scope for plenty of discussion, racial interaction and a bit of good old-fashioned flag-waving. The only trouble was Crawfords weren't happy with any of the aboriginal actresses who auditioned and decided to use a white actress, Marina Finlay, under a layer of burnt cork.

Word got out and the proverbial fan almost jammed. Apart from the justifiably angry reaction from aborigines and the predictable hysteria from do-gooders, Actors' Equity just wouldn't cop it. The script was re-written to make the heroine a white woman sympathetic to the aboriginal cause. Actors' Equity grudgingly accepted the compromise but it left a bitter taste on a lot of already bitter tongues.

The next attempt was far more successful. Aboriginal actress Kylie Belling, fresh from an acting course with the Victorian College of Arts, was cast to play Sharon Herbert, a bright, fresh-faced teenager later to become a regular in the series. Rather than treat her as an aborigine first and an individual second, the sort of tokenism which Australian television and cinema has long been guilty of, the Crawford team allowed her to meld into the township as a real person, colour accepted and taken for granted as one of them. As Kylie says: 'The question of race eventually does come up but I'm protected from the racists by everyone in town and in fact, I have to go as far as asserting my aboriginality.'

Kylie was discovered by director Bruce Beresford when he was casting *The Fringe Dwellers*, to be shot in Queensland. Kylie was brought up as one of three adopted aborigines by a white family in Melbourne. As far as racial conflict is concerned, Queensland is to Australia what Mississippi is to the United States. As a 'southerner' and an aborigine plucked from a college education, Kylie was deeply apprehensive about her reception in Queensland. Worse than that, she'd never had much contact with people of her own race, so she'd have to rely for protection on a bunch of film people who'd probably spend all their spare time in the pub anyhow.

'It all worked out fine. Everyone was polite and friendly, especially Bruce Beresford. He really is an actor's director. He has a very good understanding and can home in on what actors need, nothing more and nothing less. I think I must be the luckiest girl alive, aborigine or not, to have come straight from school into a major feature film directed by one of the world's greatest. And now, with *The Flying Doctors* I've got an even better chance to develop my acting skills without having to worry about those stupid racial attitudes.'

Kylie also had the good luck to be under the wing of the patriarch of the Australian television industry, Hector Crawford, dubbed 'The Silver Fox' because of his flowing mane of steel-grey hair. Crawford died in March 1991 after a long battle with illnesses ranging from cancer to heart attacks.

It is more than fifty years since Crawford produced his first radio documentary, but even then he was reaching for the top – the show was about one of Australia's most famous women, Dame Nellie Melba, some say the greatest soprano who ever lived. He founded the country's first independent televison production house and since then his list of credits reads like a living history of Australian television, from *Homicide* through *The Sullivans* to *The Flying Doctors*, which he regarded as one of his finest efforts and right to the end, watched over it like a fox over its young. He once threatened legal action against a Sydney production team which wanted to produce a series called *Air Doctor One* for the American market. It never went ahead but the rival producers remarked at the time: 'The only similarity is that both shows are effectively medical and medical shows are not exclusive. Remember Crawford Productions had three cop shows (*Homicide*, *Division Four* and *Matlock*) on different Australian networks at the same time.' It probably says as much about 'The Silver Fox' as a truckload of screen credits and balance sheets.

Whether he had a great eye for untested talent, or the inevitable success of his shows ensured their stardom, Hector Crawford cultivated and launched more actors and performers into celebrity status than any other Australian. He was also a major force in building up the pro-

ducing, directing, writing and technical talent which was ready and waiting when the Australian film renaissance took hold. These days his son, Ian, is managing director but as the cameras whir, the ghost of the old fox still lopes through the backdrops.

Another experiment in realism was to take one of Australia's leading young comics, George Kapiniaris, and give him a straight role as the local RFDS radio operator. The role is played with plenty of fast talking and live-wire antics – he's named DJ for disc jockey – but underneath he can handle an emergency with the best of them. Said Kapiniaris, who holds a Bachelor of Arts in Drama and Media studies: 'I enjoy going under the title of an actor. A comic is an actor who plays comedy. He can be a singer, part of a cabaret show, a television show or a film. All the time people expect you to be funny. *The Flying Doctors* comes as a relief because the pressure is off. On the set, the jokes spring from other cast members such as Peter O'Brien and Maurie Fields. They're blokes we really respect.'

From the episode 'A Painful Extraction', a farewell to DJ (second on the left), played by young comedian George Kapiniaris

George's comedy show, *Acropolis Now*, is also a piece of social realism in its way. It takes a crack at all the holy cows associated with cultural integration and sends up Australian-Greeks as much as Australians. 'That's where you really get the pressure. People come up and say, "Tell us a joke. Go on." So you pick a joke like, "Why are Greeks really bad at soccer? Because every time they get a corner they put a milk bar on it." They usually look uncomfortable and go away.'

Equally unlikely was the casting of another Australian-Greek, football superstar, Robert Dipierdomenico. Known as 'The Big Dipper' to his Australian Rules fans (a game that has its origins in Irish football, where players handle the ball and kick goals through un-netted goal posts from enormous distances), he plays a drug-crazed truck driver who hears on citizens' band radio that his luscious, hitch-hiking girlfriend Vanessa is shacked up with mild-mannered Dr Geoff Standish. What follows is a *High Noon* stand-off in the deserted main street of Coopers Crossing where 'The Big Dip' takes a wild swing at Dr Geoff and is laid out cold with a neat right. It turns out he was packed to the gills with illegal substances and once they'd detoxicated him, 'The Big Dip' disappeared into the dusty sunset with Vanessa.

Well, rules are made to be broken and these little tongue-in-cheek lapses are so well done they tend to enliven life in Coopers Crossing rather than turn it into the sound stage of *Die Hard*. As Maurie Fields remarked: 'In this business you can fool some of the people some of the time, but you better leave it at that.'

The Flying Doctors leaves it at that. And in many ways has brushed the soap bubbles from Australian television. Its success in Europe and its ability to hook devoted fans, means the formula is working and as long as they don't mess with it, will continue to work. As Crawford's Chief Executive Officer, Terry Ohlsson, remarked: 'The ingredients are there, the audience is there and I can't see any reason why this show couldn't last well into the next century.'

Coronation Street and *EastEnders*, look out!